Peppers Hot & Chile

Peppers Hot & Chile

A Cook's
Guide to
Chile
Peppers
from California,
the Southwest,
Mexico,
and Beyond

Georgeanne Brennan and Charlotte Glenn

Aris Books

▲▲ Addison-Wesley Publishing Company, Inc.

Reading, Massachusetts   Menlo Park, California   New York
Don Mills, Ontario   Wokingham, England   Amsterdam   Bonn
Sydney   Singapore   Tokyo   Madrid   San Juan

Library of Congress Cataloging-in-Publication Data

Brennan, Georgeanne, 1943–
  Peppers hot & chile: a cook's guide to chile peppers from California, the Southwest, Mexico, and beyond/Georgeanne Brennan and Charlotte Glenn.
     p.   cm.—(Kitchen edition)
  Includes index.
  ISBN 0-201-17019-1
  1. Cookery (Hot peppers) 2. Hot peppers. I. Glenn, Charlotte, 1943–   . II. Title. III. Title: Peppers hot and chile.
IV. Series.
TX803.P46B74 1988
641.6'384—dc19   88-29414

Kitchen Edition books are published by Aris Books, an imprint of Addison-Wesley Publishing Company, Inc.

Aris Books Editorial Offices and Test Kitchen
1621 Fifth Street
Berkeley, CA 94710
(415) 527-5171

Series Editor: John Harris
Project Editor: Lee Mooney
Consulting Editor: S. Irene Virbila
Series Design: Lynne O'Neil
Cover Photo: Lisa Blevins
Food Stylist: Stevie Bass
Illustrations: Pamela Manley
Set in 10 point Baskerville by Another Point, Inc., Oakland, CA

BCDEFGHIJ—DO—89
Second Printing, May 1989

Contents

A Pepper Guide:
Use this map to identify the items that appear on the cover.

1. Ancho chile
2. Negro chile
3. New Mexico chile
4. Guajillo chile
5. Poblano chile
6. Cherry pepper
7. Jalapeno chile
8. Serrano chile
9. Hungarian wax pepper
10. Serrano chile
11. Japones chiles
12. Anaheim chile
13. New Mexico chile powder
14. Pequin chile
15. Paprika
16. Fish Poached in Poblano Sauce (recipe on page 38)

Foreword

The genesis of *Peppers Hot and Chile* was a series of classes we taught at the Aris Test Kitchen in the summer of 1986. What we did then, and repeat in this book, was to discuss the traditional and not so traditional uses of fresh and dried chiles. This means that our recipes make use of chile peppers and not other kinds of peppers, such as bell peppers. This is not another Mexican cookbook, or Tex-mex cookbook, although there are references to Mexican and Southwestern treatments of chiles and other ingredients. This cookbook is a primer for the cook interested in furthering his or her working knowledge of chiles, and we hope it will inspire cooks to incorporate chiles into their present style of food preparation.

In writing *Peppers Hot and Chile*, we have been caught in the "Spanglish" dilemma in which so many Hispanics in the United States find themselves: when to use English and when to use Spanish, and should they be combined. For example, should salsas be called sauces and even more importantly, should chiles be spelled with an *i* as in the English version or with an *e* as per Spanish spelling. Round and round we've gone, finally realizing that indeed our Western language is truly a blending of both English and Spanish terms. We chose the traditional Hispanic spelling of chile as it reflects our Western roots, but then we sometimes call cooked salsas sauces. All this has caused our editors to ask a number of questions and for all of us to reflect on the fact that our language is ever-changing. As a point of style we have not marked the tildes or accents traditionally found in some Hispanic words, as in jalapeno or arbol.

We hope you use this book, scribble notes to yourselves in the margins, perhaps even draw the shape of a "new" chile you've spotted at the local supermarket.

Even before a single word was written people were enthusiastic about *Peppers Hot and Chile*. Neighborhood friends, Mr. and Mrs. Martinez, shared their special home garden chiles with us. Marta and Letetcia Gonzales contacted their extended family throughout California and Mexico for recipes and techniques. Jose Luis brought us sacksful of habaneros from his Dixon backyard. Classes began at the Aris Test Kitchen in Berkeley. While we demonstrated techniques, Stephen and Nancy Glenn and Ethel Brennan toasted chiles and chopped ingredients for us. Kari Lester helped too. Maryanne Pohl supplied us on a moment's notice with whatever ingredient happened to be missing. Once classes finished, cooking and writing continued in Dixon. Our Le Marché employees, Reyes Hague, Marta Gonzales, Ann Katz, Tina Smith and Stacey Gleason cooked dishes taken from the book in progress and served them at food events. Shelly Hird and Pepe Barrajas lent their expertise to the tamale section. Jim Ver Steeg and Jim Schrupp read the first complete manuscript and gave us thoughtful comments and criticisms. Visiting professor, Jose le Borde, encouraged us throughout and gave us technical assistance. John Glenn was always at hand to answer computer questions as changes were made. Oliver Brennan, Tom and Dan Schrupp were willing samplers for the final go round of recipe testing. Carrie Sharkey and Donna Haile typed the final manuscript. Our editors, John Harris, Lee Mooney and Sherry Virbila have been unfailingly supportive.

The seeds and ribs inside the chile are the source of its heat.

 HOT FLASH!

When you see this pepper symbol next to a recipe title, it means the dish will be very hot.

Caution: Handling Hot Chiles

The flesh of a chile is not hot. The heat comes from *capsaicin*, which is present in the seeds and in the ribs that hold the seeds. If you remove the seeds and ribs, the pepper's intensity will be markedly reduced.

When handling any hot peppers, use caution. We recommend using rubber gloves when working with peppers. It's not just biting into a pepper that can produce heat; handling the skin and then licking your fingers will burn your tongue as much as a bite of the pepper itself. Also be careful not to rub your eyes after handling peppers. Grinding chiles can also cause some irritation. Be sure to turn on your kitchen fan or open a window when grinding chiles.

For a more extensive discussion of the principles underlying chile hotness, and how to work with these elements in your cooking, see page 84.

Introduction

The chile pepper is an international figure, sought after by cooks in regional markets in the temperate and tropical world. Chiles grow abundantly in parts of Asia, India, Europe and the Americas, although they are native to tropical and subtropical America. True chile country extends from Mexico in the north to Bolivia in South America.

In the last 10 years an increasing number of chiles, both fresh and dried, have been appearing in produce and specialty sections of supermarkets across the United States, not just in "chile territory," and the trend is continuing. Unfortunately, information about these chiles has not kept pace with availability of the chiles themselves. Just what does one do with a dried chile? Are salsas made with fresh chiles or dried ones or both? Are chile rellenos always made with a certain kind of chile? Are there any shortcuts to moles and stews or do they always take a long time? Can chiles be ground up in a blender or only in a *molcajete* (see page 24)? This book is an attempt to answer these questions as well as many others and to make the chiles easily accessible to anyone who likes to cook.

The word "chile" is derived from the Nahuatl dialect of Central Mexico, the ancestral home of the Aztec Indians. "Chil" meant chile, and today in Mexico, as in the United States, hot peppers are called chiles. In Mexico, sweet peppers are known as *pimientos dulces*. You may recall the story about Christopher Columbus, who took to the seas in search of India and would-be treasures like the spice black pepper. So when he found "Indians" with chiles, he named the fruits pimientos, or peppers. Most Europeans call the hot pepper "hot capsicums," although the British prefer "chilli." This brings up the point of the correct way to spell chile. The *e* ending, chile, is the authentic Hispanic spelling of the word, whereas English linguists have changed the *e* to an *i*, most probably because phonetically the *i* is more true in sound for English speakers. The British generally spell the word with a double *l*.

After Columbus' time, chiles quickly found their way into the cuisines of the world. The chile not only provided a zesty new flavor to traditional foods, but it also was used to preserve dishes and ingredients that easily spoiled. There is also some evidence that chiles may have addictive qualities, so that the adage "once a chile lover, always a chile lover" may have had some long-enduring effect on why chiles were incorporated into cuisines that for centuries did without them. Spicy walnut chicken of southern China, hot bean paste, Mongolian barbeque, Thai fish broth, Hungarian goulash, Indian curries and African harissa are but a few well-known dishes that call for chiles.

But the New World seems to be the center of genetic diversity of the chile and of its uses in regional cooking. One finds chiles used not only as spice but also as a main ingredient. Chiles, used as a primary ingredient, contribute flavor, texture and color to the dish at hand, as well as nutrition. Mature chiles are full of vitamin C and iron. Chile salsas—or sauces—are so common in Mexico that they are taken for granted. In California a Mexican restaurant is quickly evaluated by the quality of its salsas, and trendy salsa bars may either "make it" or not depending upon their salsas. Toasted, chopped green serranos with tomatillos, finely diced jalapenos with raw tomatoes, and red sauce of dried anchos simmered to a full-bodied richness are among the salsas that typically adorn table-tops.

Botanically, the chile peppers belong to one large genus called *Capsicum.* This group includes sweet peppers as well as chiles. Most of the commercially available chiles also belong to a more specific unit, *Capsicum annuum.* However, there are a few exceptions. The habanero chile of the Yucatan peninsula is *Capsicum sinense.* The tabasco pepper, which has helped to make Creole cooking famous is *Capsicum frutescens.* The bird pepper of Southeast Asia, is thought to be Capsicum, although there is some disagreement on the classification. Perhaps the point here is that while there are a great number of unusual peppers (to those of us in the United States), commercially we largely see variations of *Capsicum annuum.*

Chile names are elusive, however. Just when you think you have them categorized and have matched names with physical appearances, you are introduced to a new form. In Mexico alone it is said there are over sixty-five various kinds of chiles, many of which reflect only subtle differences from one another. The conditions under which chile plants are grown may be responsible for some variation, but genetic isolation and selection of basically similar plants over the years may also be causes for differences from one region to another.

By their very nature chiles vary in color, shape and texture, as well as in hotness and flavor. There are some constant characteristics, however. When the fruits are first formed, most chiles are green, and, with the onset of maturity, change to brilliant red. Others, as they ripen, change to yellow, orange, salmon and even chocolate brown. But they start out shades lighter.

Their shapes truly vary. You may find the tiny tepins, about the size of your fingertips, fresh in the markets of the American Southwest, or the round cherry types at roadside stands in mid-America. Tubular chiles, which may be elegantly smooth or very wrinkled, such as the cayenne, Chimayo, and Hungarian wax, grow in just about every possible warm place in the United States. You will find them in most summer markets scattered throughout the country. Then there are the puffy types such as the pasilla/poblano and mulato, so typical of the Southwest and of Mexico. Smooth-skinned or rough, even striated from the intense sun, all kinds of chiles are presented to consumers.

As you search for chiles in produce markets, you're apt to find yellow and green chiles, and perhaps some red ones. More than likely the chiles will be sold under names such as "Long Green Chile" (Anaheim or New Mexico), "Green Chile" (serrano or jalapeno), and "Yellow Chile" (yellow wax or guerro). Small red chiles may be cayenne, arbol, Thai, bird's eye, or a close strain of any one of these. Large red chiles may be labeled as "Colorados" or simply "Red Chiles."

In regional or ethnic markets more specific epithets may be applied, but they often vary from place to place or by season. They may vary because the chile suppliers have changed, and although the chiles are the same, the names are not. Don't be disheartened—in time you will learn to recognize chiles, how they flavor various dishes and which ones work best for you.

Dried chiles are now marketed by a surprising number of distributors, and there are many different kinds. The range of availability is greater with the dried chiles at this point than with the fresh ones, and you will learn after handling and cooking with dried chiles which kinds you like to use.

The American cook's interest in exotic ingredients is at an all time high point, and the chile pepper (whether hot or mild) measures up to this demand for new tastes. And, we are not talking about *chili* (e.g. *chili con carne*), that ubiquitous stew of beans, meat and chili powder. As our country becomes home to an increasingly diverse ethnic population, the demand for authentic ingredients will continue, and these ingredients will make their way into the foods of the general population. We expect that the standard preparations like chili, or the bland dishes we find in most Mexican restaurants will slowly give way to authentic dishes of more taste, spice and heat.

Illustrated Chile Pepper Glossary

There are at least twenty kinds of chiles commercially available in the United States. In some regions, such as the Southwest and Southeast, one might find at least a dozen of these at one market alone. In less familiar territory a shopper might be lucky to spot one green and one yellow chile. However, with the trend in market sophistication and increased demand for diversity, soon an increasing number of chiles will be found on produce shelves in all regions of the country.

Some commonly found chiles are listed below with a brief description of their distinguishing characteristics.

Anaheim *(also known as New Mexico, long red chile, long green chile, Texas chile, or, when dried, as California, New Mexico, Colorado and sometimes guajillo)*

The Anaheim group is pale to medium green and only mildly piquant. Its fruits are six to eight inches long, tapering to a point from narrow shoulders. This group is known as the best stuffing chile in the United States. It is also frequently used in salsas and casseroles, especially when canned. At maturity Anaheims turn bright red. Substitute bell peppers or Italian peppers if necessary.

Ancho *(dried)* See Poblano.

Arbol *(also known as a type of cayenne, and in some localities as the Chimayo, or even Thai or bird chile)*

Slender, tubular, slightly curving pods, two to three inches long, characterize the arbol. It can be bitingly hot without much distinctive flavor. When first formed the chile is bright green, but with maturity turns bright red. The arbol may be used either fresh, green or red, or dried when mature.

Bird See Thai.

California *(dried)* See Anaheim.

Cascabel *(dried)* See Cherry Pepper.

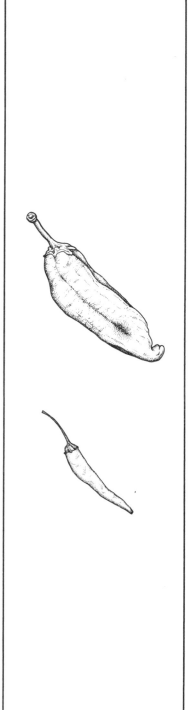

Cayenne *(see Arbol for other names)*

Any number of strains of red and green chiles may be seen in local marketplaces. They are typically slender, tubular, often slightly wrinkled and curving, with pods up to four inches long. Cayennes are hot, but not distinctive. Use them whenever fresh chiles are called for. Substitute mature Anaheims, although cayennes are typically smaller and hotter than Anaheims. Cayennes are frequently dried.

Cherry Pepper *(also known as hot cherry pepper, but not chile)*

The small round, somewhat flattened green and red peppers with diameters about the size of quarters are frequently pickled and served in gardiniera, a mixture of pickled vegetables. Cherry peppers are not very hot, having only a spicy piquancy, which makes them a fresh alternative in salads and salsas. The dried cascabel bears a resemblance to the cherry.

Chilaca See Pasilla.

Chimayo See Arbol.

Chipotle

Most typically seen in canned form in the United States, the hot chipotle is really a smoked jalapeno that has taken on a charred flavor while drying. In a dried state, chipotles are roughly textured and warm brown in color. Because they are fragile, most are preserved in a vinegar solution to which garlic and tomatoes may be added.

Colorado *(dried)* See Anaheim.

Fresno

Tapered, but rather short, not over one and one-half inches, this waxy pepper is usually harvested in its immature state, when pale green. It is not particularly hot. Substitute serranos.

Guajillo *(dried)* See Anaheim.

Guerro

Not unlike the hot yellow Hungarian wax, the guerro tends to be smaller and somewhat blunter-nosed than the Hungarian. Guerros measure two inches long and are characteristically pale yellow. Substitute Hungarian wax chiles.

Habanero *(also referred to as King of the Yucatan)*

Immigrants from the Yucatan Peninsula like to bring with them a few seeds of this fiery hot, golden orange pepper. It is small, wrinkled and puffy, resembling a two-inch-long lantern. One habanero is enough for a great salsa. Look for bottled habanero salsa in ethnic markets. It will be either green, made from the immature fruits, or yellow. There is no substitute. When dried, the habanero turns golden brown and is rarely seen in the marketplace, although home gardeners do dry them.

Hungarian Wax

A canary yellow, turning salmon and then bright red, the Hungarian wax is three to five inches long and at least one and one-quarter inches across. It has a green pepper flavor with hotness besides. It is good for frying. Substitute guerros or Anaheims.

Jalapeno

Thick-meated, plump peppers, jalapenos turn from a shiny dark green to bright red, but they are almost always marketed in the green state. They are one to one and one-half inches long and shaped like bullets. These chiles may have sun marks, or striations, that run lengthwise down the skin and indicate high quality and heat. Although considered to be a very hot pepper, they vary in piquancy. A recent development is the Tam mild jalapeno, developed for spicy flavor with reduced hotness. Jalapenos are one of the most versatile of the chiles and can be used in almost every kind of dish. A smoked, dried jalapeno is called chipotle (see page 14), and these are required for special dishes. Substitute serranos for fresh jalapenos.

Japones *(dried)* See Thai.

Long Green See Anaheim.

Long Red See Anaheim.

Mulato See Poblano.

Negro *(dried chilaca)* See Pasilla.

New Mexico *(dried)* See Anaheim.

Paprika *(also called the tomato or box pepper, due to its shape)*

There are many paprikas, but one of the common types develops into a boxy fruit, not much larger than a tangerine. Paprikas are convoluted and wrinkled, making peeling difficult. Remove skin with a vegetable peeler or leave skin intact. Fresh, the paprika makes a good stuffing pepper with its thick, meaty walls. It has the bell pepper flavor with a little piquancy. Since the seeds, ground into powder, are the normal product of this pepper, you will find whole paprikas only as a specialty item. Substitute bell peppers.

Pasilla *(also called chilaca chile or, when dried, negro chile)*

The true pasilla is dark green, long, tapering and narrow, with a blunt end. In Baja California, where much produce is grown and then shipped throughout the United States, the poblano is labeled as pasilla. Consequently, in California markets one can find two types of chiles vying for the name pasilla—the true pasilla as described above, and the poblano, which is a heavier, more broad-shouldered cousin. The pasilla is used in meat entrées, tamales and quesadillas. Dried, under the name of negro chile, it renders a thick, rich, dark sauce. Substitute poblanos for pasillas; they are both mild to medium hot.

Pequin

This tiny, hot chile is normally sold dried, but it is sometimes found fresh in roadside stands and at farmers' markets. Pequins grow wild in many mountainous areas of Mexico.

Pimiento

Heart-shaped and deep red, about the size of a child's fist, the pimiento is not always sweet, contrary to popular opinion. These red peppers may be used where only a very mild piquancy is desired. With their thick skin and heavy flesh, they are good for stuffing or substituting for Anaheim types.

Poblano *(also called pasilla; mulato is a kind of poblano)*

Puffy and large, the three-inch-wide stem end tapers to a pointed tip. Also dark green, poblanos range in size from three to five inches long, and are used for rellenos and for making rich, thick sauces. The poblano is the chile most California-style restaurants use and call pasilla. Mexicans identify the pasilla as the slender, tubular chile (see Pasilla entry). Don't worry much about the name—it is worth finding a source for this mild to medium chile and using it as often as you can. The mulato is the same type, as is the ancho, but these are almost always dried.

Serrano *(sometimes labeled green chile)*

This medium-green chile looks like a bullet, one and one-half inches long and three-quarters of an inch in diameter. It is not as meaty as the jalapeno. You can distinguish it from the jalapeno by holding the two side by side. The jalapeno will always look smooth and polished, while the serrano lacks full luster. It has a thin skin and medium amount of meat. The veins and seeds of the serrano are especially hot and, depending upon tastes, can be used or discarded. The serrano, like the jalapeno, is very versatile.

Tepin

Smaller even than the tiny pequin, about the size of your smallest fingernail, these hot chiles are also found fresh occasionally and are used for flavoring soups and stews.

Texas See Anaheim.

Thai *(also known as bird chile, and when dried, as japones)*

With slender, pointed pods that are usually straight, the Thai chile resembles the arbol and shares its heat as well. It is distinguished from the arbol by its more solid walls. It is green when immature and red at full maturity.

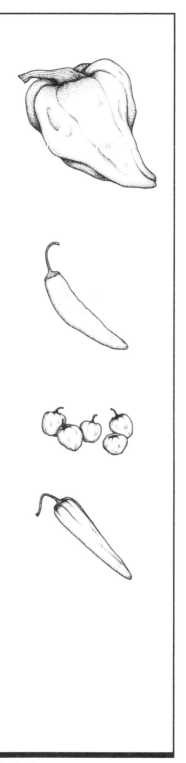

Growing Your Own Chiles

One of the fascinating things about chiles is their tremendous diversity. In the United States we see commercially only a very few of the many, many different kinds of peppers, both fresh and dried.

Most of us are familiar now with some of the sweet peppers, the bell types which come in many colors — red, green, yellow, even purple, brown and white. The long, thick Lamuyo or European bell-type peppers are more available now. On the East Coast especially, markets carry many of the sweet frying peppers which have tapered ends and look more like cones than bells.

The world of hot chiles is much more diverse, yet we see even less of it. The huge variety of chiles is really only readily available south of the border, in Mexico, along the border states and in some speciality markets in the West.

Those of us without access to all these will have to content ourselves with the most common fresh chiles: serranos, jalapenos, Anaheims, hot yellow wax, and an occasional pasilla/poblano. Most likely we can get others in a dried form from mail-order sources, even if they are not readily available in the markets.

But what if you could grow chiles in your own garden? It would mean you could try your hand at varieties of your own choosing and you could pick the chiles at their prime condition. You don't need lots of space, and the growing conditions are made simple with "season extenders." With cloches, plastic tunnels, mulches, southern exposure and greenhouses, whatever growing conditions are required can be created. Contrary to popular opinion, chiles do not need searing hot days to produce. In fact, extreme heat can inhibit fruiting. What chiles do need is very warm soil temperatures for germination, as high as 80 degrees; moderately warm days, 80 to 95 degrees; and nights in the 55 to 70 degree range. If you don't have these conditions naturally, you can create them with artificial means, such as grow lights. Remember, some of the finest chiles are grown on the high plateaus of Central Mexico, Arizona and New Mexico, where temperatures are rarely above 85 degrees. Most likely you will need to increase your season of "good days" by starting seedlings inside during the cold months of the northern spring. Varieties such as serrano, jalapeno, hot wax and some Anaheims will mature more quickly than pasillas and poblanos. Count on ninety-five days after transplanting for your first chiles to mature.

Germination

Start inside. Select either flats or pots and fill with a commercial potting mix. Punch in seeds that have been pre-soaked. Soaking overnight in hot water helps break the dormancy which often inhibits pepper seeds from germinating. Cover the seeds with a bare one-quarter inch of soil pressed firmly over the top, and space at least two inches apart. Keep your flats or pots moist and warm. Try keeping them on top of a warm appliance, such as the hot-water heater or the clothes dryer, until germination occurs.

Early Growth

Once the pepper plants have four leaves, they will need some light as well as warmth. If your appliance-top location can provide these conditions, or if you can install an artificial grow light there, leave them right there. If not, the seedlings will need a new location. The new location can be inside or outside in a plastic greenhouse, under glass, or any other arrangement that keeps the soil warm, the air temperature in the optimum range, and provides plenty of light.

Transplanting

As the plants mature, they will need fertilizer, specifically, nitrogen, phosphorous and potassium. This can be supplied by a commercial mix. Read the directions carefully on the fertilizer you choose, making sure that it will not burn young plants. When all danger of frost has passed in your area, the days and nights have warmed, and the soil feels warm to your touch, plant your little seedlings in your garden. Or, if you wish, you can continue to raise them in your greenhouse. Many farmers in the wonderful climate and soils of southern France continue to grow their peppers throughout the summer in small greenhouses and manage to have a supply almost year round. Some gardeners we know have chile plants that are several years old. However, many of us like to use the greenhouse when we have to propagate the next group of seedlings.

When placing chile plants in their final location in a garden bed, space the plants twenty-four inches apart from each other in a row, and keep rows at least thirty inches apart. Other spacings are possible, but these will give your plants plenty of room. Some varieties do grow larger than others, and pruning is recommended for plants that become too bushy.

In the open garden space, put a paper collar around your plants if chewing insects are a problem, or a water collar for thermal insulation.

Hints

If your days are hot when you transplant, give your seedlings protection. Set up a shade, either a broken tree branch with leaves intact or a shade cloth, for each plant.

Watch your plants carefully for water needs. If you see the leaves drooping and looking lusterless, water them. You'll be surprised how quickly they respond.

Harvesting

This is the best part. Harvest your chiles early in the morning when the plant is most supple. Using clippers, cut each chile, leaving a one-quarter to one-half inch stem on each fruit. Remember that chiles change color and flavor as they mature, so you may want to begin harvesting at the green stage, then again throughout the maturation period. If you keep picking the fruits, chiles will continue to fruit until autumn. Some chiles are almost flavorless at the green stage (Thai, cayenne types and paprikas), while others are considered at their best (jalapenos, Anaheims, pasilla/poblanos and serranos). Thai, cayenne and paprika chiles are best when deep red.

Drying Chiles

Fully mature red or yellow chiles are the most suitable for drying. Immature chiles may mold or turn brown when dried. Chiles may be dried by placing them on screens or stringing and then hanging them. Screens work well as they permit air to circulate under the chiles, but if you notice moisture collecting beneath them, you should turn them over to hasten drying and to prevent mold build-up.

If you choose to string your chiles, use a yarn needle and heavy cotton thread. Puncture each chile at its cap (*calyx*), just below the stem, and string as you would cranberries and pop-corn for the holidays. Suspend your line of chiles under the eaves of your house or in a breezeway—anywhere warm air will move by them. In late summer when days are 85 degrees and not humid, the chiles will dry in a week. If you live where the air is humid, plan on using a food dehydrator or a warm place inside.

Storing Chiles

Once dry, chiles may be placed in self-sealing plastic bags and stored in the freezer, or put in sealable storage containers and held at room temperature. Some cooks prefer to keep strings of chiles, called ristras, close to the kitchen work space.

Special Ingredients and Utensils

Achiote is found in paste or powder form in market places of southern Mexico. The red seeds of the annatto tree are ground and pulverized and used as a carrier for additional seasonings. Ground, dried chiles as well as spices and herbs are added to achiote and each vendor sells his own special blend. The red coloring of achiote used in fish, fowl or red meat dishes adds a strong luster.

Adobo is a savory sauce that is hard to resist since it incorporates a hearty chile flavor, herbs such as cumin and oregano, and vinegar or lime juice. It is often a carrier for meat and vegetable main dishes.

Chocolate (Mexican) can be found in specialty stores as well as large supermarkets. The most common brand is Ibarra. Mexican chocolate contains roughly textured sugar granules and is designed to be heated with milk for sweet beverages. Its flavor is distinctive.

Cilantro, also known as Chinese parsley and coriander, is an herb with feathery green parsley-shaped leaves and bears pale lavender flowers. The seed, known as the spice coriander, is also used in cooking. Cilantro may be used raw or cooked.

Comal is the griddle put over the open flame used for toasting chiles, tomatillos, and other vegetables, and for baking tortillas and other masa products. An immensely useful tool, the comal may be as simple as a thin piece of sheet iron or an expensive heavy piece of cast iron. In some areas a heavy pottery is also used. Any flat-surfaced griddle or frying pan that can be thoroughly heated (to the smoking point) is a good substitute for a comal.

Corn husks (hojas): See Tamale wrappers.

Crema mexicana is a thick cultured sour cream which may be purchased in specialty shops or Hispanic markets. It is thicker and richer than standard sour cream. Substitute ordinary sour cream or crème fraîche.

Crème fraîche is a thick cream made by adding 2 tablespoons buttermilk to ½ cup heavy cream and letting it age overnight. It has a nutty, slightly sour flavor and is perfect for sauces that need to be reduced, since crème fraîche does not separate when heated.

Elote is the name given to corn, both the ear of fresh corn and the stamens that are removed from the ear of corn and dried for use in teas. Elote is sometimes called Mexican saffron because the dried stamens yield an orange-red dye when placed in water. The dried stamens themselves may be added to foods such as rice, just like saffron.

Epazote, also written **apazote,** is a strongly flavored green herb used in making bean stews, soups, and fillings for quesadillas. Epazote grows easily from seed in areas where days and nights are warm. It will not tolerate the cold nor drought. The notched leaves resemble mint, but the plant is a wormseed of the Chenopodium species. Its flavor is a cross between aromatic resin and mint.

Escabeche is the name applied to a vinegar sauce that is typically seasoned with chiles and salt. In the United States you can find *jalapenos en escabeche* or recipes that call for a dash of this fiery substance.

Fresh ginger root, found nationally in most supermarkets, is easily recognized as a tan or light brown rhizome shaped like a hand. It is easy to use. It may be peeled, grated and chopped, or pureed in a food processor. Ginger root may also be frozen and partially used, then returned to the freezer. Ginger root is subject to molding, so inspect the pieces carefully. The "root" is actually a rhizome.

Huitlacoche is the name given to kernels of corn that have become distorted by a fungus. The infected kernels swell and become a glistening bluish silver color. Inside the kernel is a bluish black powder. Huitlacoche is considered a great delicacy in many areas of Mexico, and innovative American chefs are beginning to experiment with it. It is quite perishable and consequently not readily available.

Jicama is a succulent tan-skinned tuber that looks like a round potato. Its smooth surface should not be pitted and the entire vegetable should be firm, not soft or mushy. To use jicama, peel it and slice in rounds, dice or grate. Its flesh is crunchy and, when fresh, starchy sweet. It will keep up to a week in the refrigerator. If you cannot find jicama, water chestnuts are the best substitute.

Masa refers to the meal used for making dough, either *masa de harina* or *masa de maiz*. Harina is wheat flour and maiz is corn. The dough of either one has many uses, although the primary uses are for tortillas and tamales. Masa may also be used as a thickening agent, just as flour or cornstarch.

Molcajete is an indispensable hand utensil found in most Mexican kitchens. It is a mortar, usually made of basalt or granite, which is used for grinding chiles, spices and herbs. It also becomes the basin for making salsas. After the grinding operation, tomatoes, tomatillos, or other ingredients are added to the molcajete for final blending.

Mole is the sauce of central Mexico known in the United States as a combination of chocolate and other seasonings. The word mole means concoction, and a typical mole may have as many as ten or more ingredients, including pumpkin seeds, cloves, allspice, peanuts, almonds or sesame seeds, lettuce or chocolate as well as chiles and broth of turkey, chicken or duck. *Mole verde* is a green mole sauce made with lettuce and cilantro, and not chocolate. *Mole de olla*, a popular kind of mole and well known outside of Mexico, is translated as "mole in a pot" and it generally contains chocolate.

Pepitos are pumpkin seeds that are usually removed from their kernels, toasted and salted, if eaten as a snack food. If used as an ingredient in cooking, they are sold either raw or toasted, but not salted.

Pipian sauce is a mixture containing nuts or seeds, but it is far less complicated than mole. Pipians generally contain five or six ingredients and always incorporate ground nuts and seeds which yield the predominating flavor.

Queso means cheese. There are many kinds of Mexican cheeses. We have listed four types that we find most useful.

Queso anejo is a type of cheese that is dry, salty, and very white. It is not unlike feta, but feta contains more moisture. Queso anejo is used crumbled as a topping for many casserole and bean dishes and also for enchiladas.

Queso asadero is much like string cheese. It is packed either in long strands or in round balls, with the stringy ropes wound up like a ball of yarn. Use queso asadero any way you would a low-moisture mozzarella or string cheese. In Mexico it is used extensively in quesadillas.

Queso cotija is another crumbly white cheese similar to anejo (some even say it is the same). Use it in the same manner as queso anejo.

Queso fresco is a white, fresh farmer cheese that is often added to salads or tacos at the last moment. It has a mild flavor since it has not been allowed to age.

Rice wine vinegar is a mildly aromatic, sparkling gold vinegar from Japan that may be purchased unseasoned or seasoned with sugar, salt and monosodium glutamate, among other ingredients. We recommend the unseasoned type for the recipes in this book.

Rocket, also known as roquette and arugula, is a spicy Italian green used in its small state as a salad green and when mature as a braising green or wrapper.

Tamale wrappers are used to hold together the dough and filling. The most common wrappers are dried corn husks which are sold either packaged or loose in many markets. If they are unavailable, you can dry your own (see page 45). Bamboo, sisal, banana, grape and fig leaves are also used as tamale wrappers.

Tomatillos, also known as *tomates verdes,* are husk tomatoes. Most found in this country are the large type, up to one and one-half inches in diameter. They are generally light green, covered with a tan parchment husk and a bit sticky. The fruit turns yellow with purple blushes at full maturity. The husks need to be removed before using in any recipe. Tomatillos may be eaten raw or cooked.

Wonton wrappers are generally made from rice flour and used for wrapping any number of ingredients, but especially mixtures for soups or deep frying. The filling is placed slightly off-center on the wrapper, the edges are folded over and sealed with water or egg. Wonton wrappers are available in most supermarkets, and they may be frozen for future use.

Cooking with Fresh Chiles

In Mexico and the southwestern United States it is traditional to use some chiles fresh and others only dried. Some chiles, like the arbol, are commonly used both ways. The chiles most frequently used fresh are serranos, jalapenos, yellow wax, Anaheims and poblanos. Sometimes they are used raw, as in salsas, but usually they are roasted first. Roasting not only helps to remove the skins, but also gives a distinctly smoky flavor to the chiles, adding another dimension to the dish in which they are used.

When using fresh, raw chiles, remember that the seeds and the ribs contain most of the capsaicin—or heat—while the distinctive flavor is found in the meat. Be cautious and protect yourself as suggested on page 8. Sometimes you may want to incorporate a few seeds into the dish you are making, but generally it is preferable to remove both seeds and ribs before using the chiles.

Raw chiles are most frequently used chopped in salsas, whole with a stuffing, or whole as a flavoring. Raw serranos, jalapenos and chile arbols are used for salsa and as flavor intensifiers; Anaheims and poblanos are slit and used raw to stuff. Fresh chiles are generally used roasted rather than raw when a subtle flavor is desired or when the skin would interfere with the overall dish, as in Fish Poached in Poblano Sauce (page 38).

Peeling chile with a
vegetable peeler

Dipping chile in hot oil
to blister skin before
peeling

Removing Skins from Fresh Chiles

It is not necessary to roast chiles in order to remove the skin. The manner of removal will affect both the taste and the appearance of the dish.

Vegetable Peeler

Peel chile with a vegetable peeler just as you would a carrot or a potato. This works best on thick-meated chiles such as poblanos and pimientos. This is a good technique for thick-meated sweet peppers too.

Hot Oil

Heat 2½ to 3 inches of vegetable oil in a heavy-bottomed saucepan. Wash and thoroughly dry the chile. Using tongs, dip the chile into the hot oil, and submerge it completely for 5 seconds. Remove and let cool. Use a sharp knife or vegetable peeler to remove the blistered skin.

Roasting

Chiles may be roasted in any number of ways, and each method alters somewhat the taste of the finished product. Some people argue for roasting over mesquite. Others say that a quick grilling over grape prunings will produce a chile with a less pronounced southwestern taste, making it more suitable to use in French- or Italian-inspired dishes. For others, aesthetics of the palate are pushed aside for practicality—broil the chiles in a gas or electric oven until charred. Traditionalists use the comal (see page 22) to very slowly blister and bubble the skin. The flat surface contact with the hot iron griddle of the comal gives a full flavor to the entire chile.

Methods for Roasting Chiles

Using a Grill

1. Heat brazier or gas grill to medium. Flames should not be searing.
2. Place chile on grill and turn after one side is toasty brown. Do not allow it to burn.

Using a Broiler

1. Place chile on broiling rack 2 inches below flame or heat element.
2. Allow skin to bubble, then turn.

Using a Comal

1. Heat comal or griddle over medium-low heat. Do not allow it to smoke.
2. Place chile on comal or griddle. Press down with your hand or the back of a wooden spoon to keep as much surface as possible in contact with the hot iron. Turn and repeat the process.

Removing the Skin from Roasted Chiles

1. Put hot roasted chile in a plastic bag or wrap in a damp cloth. Allow the chile to sweat for 5-10 minutes or until the skin slips easily from the chile.
2. Using a small paring knife or your fingers, peel the skin under running water. Rinse.

Roasting chiles on a grill

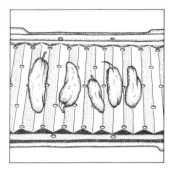

Roasting chiles under a broiler

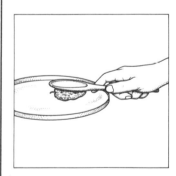

Roasting chiles on a comal

Sweating roasted chiles in a damp cloth

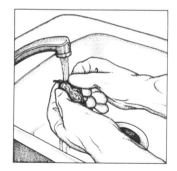

Peeling roasted chiles under running water while wearing rubber gloves

Making Chile Rellenos

One of the great delights of Mexican food is the opportunity to eat homemade rellenos (stuffed chiles). There are many kinds of rellenos, but we have come to associate the stuffed green chile batter-dipped and then deep fried as the standard. When a relleno is pulled from the fryer, blotted to remove excess oil and promptly served, topped with a cooked salsa, there is little question about how delicious it is. Homemade rellenos are generally more outstanding than most of those found in restaurants, and little wonder, as restaurants typically prepare batches of rellenos ahead of time, freeze them and then pop them into a microwave upon request.

Peppers must be thick-fleshed and large enough to hold a filling. Poblanos, mulatos and Anaheims are most commonly used, although small, sweet bells may be substituted if no chiles are to be found. Peppers must be seeded; sometimes they are also roasted and peeled before stuffing.

Care must be taken while removing the seeds. If at all possible, cut around the stem end and remove the seeds from the ribs inside. You may want to use a pair of long, slender scissors. If this procedure does not work, then you must make a slit along the side of the pepper to remove the seeds and ribs. If the slit is too large, however, the stuffing may fall out during frying.

If the recipe calls for roasting and peeling the chiles, the skin is removed. Slit the chile where desired and remove the seeds and the veins. Some recipes call for making a slit at the stem end and removing the inside contents from the top while others suggest a lengthwise slit.

The Anaheim types are traditional relleno peppers in many parts of Mexico and have been adapted into "Tex-Mex" and "Cal-Mex" cuisine in a number of forms. However, there are no absolute rules about which chile should be used for rellenos. The handling of the chiles is important, as they are somewhat fragile without their skins. Be careful not to tear, and don't overstuff. The filling is tucked inside a chile pepper—a surprise. It is not there to overpower.

Cutting around the stem end of the chile to remove the seeds and ribs

Rellenos con Queso
Cheese Rellenos

Count on a large fresh chile for each serving. Chiles are roasted and cleaned, then carefully stuffed with strips of cheese, dipped into egg batter and deep-fried.

Roast chiles using one of the methods on page 29. Peel and remove ribs and seeds. Carefully fill each chile with a strip of cheese. Reserve.

To make batter, beat egg whites separately until very stiff. Add the salt while still beating. In another bowl mix the egg yolks until lemon colored, then fold into egg whites.

To coat chiles with egg batter, choose whichever of the following methods is easiest for you: 1) Dust the peeled chile with flour, then dip it into the batter. 2) Add 2 to 3 table-spoons of flour folded into the egg mixture, then dip the stuffed chiles into the batter. 3) Skip flour altogether and dip the stuffed chiles directly into the batter. 4) Put a spoonful of batter into the hot frying oil, place the stuffed chile on top of the batter, then quickly cover the chile with another spoonful of batter.

To deep fry rellenos, heat at least 2 inches of vegetable oil in a heavy skillet or deep fryer. The ideal temperature is 375° F. With tongs place a coated chile in the hot oil. Let it cook long enough to set the batter in place. Then, roll it to begin even cooking all the way around. Because of their shapes and buoyancy you may need to hold a relleno in posi-tion to completely brown it. Total cooking time depends on the size of the chile and the density of the filling, but it is usually 2 to 3 minutes. Drain on a wire rack. Place rellenos in a warm oven until all are fried.

Serve deep-fried, batter-dipped chile rellenos with a light red salsa such as Salsa de Arbol (see page 33).

Makes 4 servings.

4 large fresh chiles, such as Anaheim or pasilla
4 ounces white cheese, such as jack, mozzarella or queso anejo, cut into 4 long pieces

BATTER
4 eggs, separated
½ tsp. salt
Flour, optional
Vegetable oil, for deep frying

RECIPE VARIATIONS

Fill each chile with 1½ to 2 tablespoons of any one of the following mix-tures instead of only cheese.

- Strips of cooked turkey or chicken alternating with the cheese
- Cooked chopped chicken mixed with pi-mientos and corn
- Refried beans seasoned with epazote or ore-gano and mixed with queso anejo
- Ground beef, sliced, black olives, and grated cheese
- Garbanzos mashed with garlic and chèvre.

Three Cheese Rellenos

*O*ne of our very favorite relleno dishes is one that doesn't require any batter or deep frying, and which also goes well with a light red salsa. This recipe calls for stuffed chiles to be simmered in crème fraîche, broth and cheese. The result is a very rich and satisfying dish.

8 roasted pasilla/
   poblano or Anaheim
   chiles
8 slices Monterey Jack
   cheese, 1 by 3 inches
   each
2 Tb. vegetable oil
1 clove garlic, minced
1 large onion, cut into
   thin slices
1½ cups chicken broth
1 cup crème fraîche
½ cup grated
   mozzarella or asadero
   cheese
2 Tb. freshly grated
   Parmesan cheese
Fresh tortillas, for
   serving

Prepare the chiles. Cut off the ends and seed. Fill each with a strip of cheese. Set aside.

Heat the oil in a heavy saucepan. Add the garlic and sauté for 1 minute. Add the onion slices. Stir-fry another minute or so. Add the chicken broth and cook for 5 minutes. Add the crème fraîche; heat; add the grated cheeses. Finally add the stuffed chiles and simmer gently for 10 minutes, long enough for the inner cheese to melt. Serve with very fresh, warm tortillas.

Makes 8 rellenos.

Making Salsas

Salsa means sauce in Spanish, but in the kitchen salsa takes on a wide range of meanings. Thick, textured salsas might even be considered relishes or condiments. There are literally dozens of salsas made from fresh raw chiles or from cooked fresh chiles. Others are made from dried chiles (which will be treated in the next chapter) or combinations of both dried and fresh chiles. Think about common dishes that may be salsa topped—eggs, tacos, tamales, tostadas, rellenos, open-face sandwiches, grilled chicken, broiled fish, simmered vegetables.

Salsa de Arbol

T his cooked salsa is an especially good accompaniment for Chile Rellenos con Queso.

Finely chop the chiles in a molcajete or with a knife. Add the garlic. Finely chop the tomatoes. Combine tomatoes with the garlic. Add the oregano. (Do not use a blender.) Heat the oil in a heavy saucepan. Add the chopped tomato mixture and cook for 5 to 10 minutes. Salt to taste.

Makes ¾ cup.

COOK'S NOTE:

Raw salsas are best used the day they are made. If you want a salsa to keep for several days, cook it after the ingredients have all been combined. While the taste will be slightly different, it will keep longer.

2 arbol chiles
1 clove garlic, minced
1½ tomatoes
2 tsp. fresh oregano
2 Tb. vegetable oil
Salt

Fresh Summer Salsa

This is a very easy salsa to make, as no cooking is required, and it is adaptable to many uses from traditional to innovative. Use it for toppings; spoon it on steamed spinach or mustard greens and serve with cornbread; turn a green salad into a taco salad by adding this salsa, cucumbers, radishes, cooked meat pieces and grated cheese.

¼ onion
3 cloves garlic, peeled
2 serrano chiles, stems removed
1 large tomato
1 Tb. chopped cilantro leaves
Juice of ⅓ lime
Salt

Grind the onion and garlic together in a blender until a paste is formed. Add the chiles and continue to grind into a paste. Add the tomato and blend, but do not puree. It should be a chunky texture. Add the cilantro. Remove to a serving bowl and add lime juice and salt to taste.

Makes 1 cup.

Salsa Verde

A mild green salsa, this one is a good choice to use with pork and chicken. It is good with both flour and corn tortillas and also makes an interesting salad dressing for either fruit or lettuce salads, especially if the salads contain citrus and dry white cheese.

10 tomatillos
1 to 2 Anaheim chiles, or, for more heat, serrano chiles
1 small onion
1 clove garlic, peeled
6 sprigs parsley or cilantro
2 Tb. vegetable oil
Salt

If fresh tomatillos are used, remove dry husks and roast them on the comal until soft. Wash and boil them in a little water until tender, about 5 to 7 minutes. If canned tomatillos are used, simply wash and drain them.

Roast green chiles and remove skins and seeds. Mince them in a blender or food processor. Add the tomatillos, onion, garlic and parsley or cilantro. Blend to a rough paste. Heat oil in skillet and cook the mixture, stirring, for 2 to 3 minutes. Add salt to taste.

Makes 1 to 1½ cups.

Habanero Salsa

Considered the king of the hot chiles by many who know the cooking of the Yucatan region of Mexico, the habanero makes a delicious hot salsa which can be used with almost any dish. Try it on a roast pork sandwich, or spooned over fresh corn cut off the cob and topped with a little cream and some chopped chorizo.

Roast the chile on a comal or on a griddle. Remove seeds and veins. Grind in a molcajete or in a blender with the garlic. Add the tomatoes and salt and pepper to taste.
   Makes 1 cup.

1 habanero chile
1 clove garlic, peeled
5 or 6 medium fresh
   summer tomatoes,
   chopped
Salt and pepper

Thai Chile Salsa

This recipe uses the very hot Thai or bird chile. The flavor is excellent, although very hot, as is the Habanero Salsa. Using it accompanied by cream will both cool and enhance the flavor. It is excellent with grilled meats.

Roast the chiles on a comal or on a griddle. Remove seeds and veins. Grind in a molcajete or in a blender with the garlic. Add the tomatoes and salt to taste and chop coarsely.
   Makes 1 cup.

6 fresh Thai chiles
2 cloves garlic, peeled
3 or 4 medium fresh
   summer or canned
   tomatoes
Salt

Green Salsa with Avocado for Barbecued Meats

*S*urprisingly rich with a lingering heat, this is an excellent accompaniment to barbecued beef and pork.

5 tomatillos
3 Hungarian wax chiles
2 serrano chiles
2 Tb. onion, chopped
1 clove garlic, minced
4 branches cilantro, minced
1 avocado, pitted and peeled
Salt

Cook tomatillos for 5 minutes in boiling water. Drain and chop. Seed, devein, and chop chiles. Combine chopped tomatillos, onion, garlic, and cilantro with chiles. Add avocado. Mash but leave chunky. Salt to taste.

Makes 1 cup.

Chile Cream Sauce

*A*nother ethnic blend, this sauce draws on French origins. This is a wonderful light yet distinctive sauce to combine with seafood—scallops or squid are good choices. Substitute tiny pieces of chile de arbol or Thai chiles for the serranos, leave them in and serve with fettuccine for a spicy adaptation.

2 shallots, peeled and minced
1 Tb. butter
4 to 6 ounces heavy cream
1 serrano chile, whole
¼ cup dry white wine
Salt

Sauté shallots in the butter. Add the cream and cook over medium heat for 8 to 10 minutes, stirring. Add the serrano chile and the wine. Continue to cook over medium heat, stirring frequently, until the sauce has reduced by at least one quarter. Salt to taste. Remove chile. Add main ingredient, such as seafood, and serve over pasta or rice.

Makes 1 scant cup sauce.

Whole Mushrooms in Green Sauce

*A*lthough *it is always tempting to use wild mushrooms or exotics such as shiitake, the standard white button mushrooms are quite delicious in this recipe. They absorb the chile and seasonings without competing or clashing with them. This is an interesting and unusual side dish or first course.*

Mince one garlic clove. Cook the onion and minced garlic in oil until onion is transparent. Add the mushrooms and the chiles, stirring well. Continue to cook until the chiles are just slightly browned and the mushrooms are golden.

Halve the tomatillos, then liquify them in a blender with the remaining garlic clove, cumin and salt to taste. Add this mixture to the mushrooms and cook over low heat for 20 minutes, allowing the mushrooms to absorb the flavors and seasonings. Especially good served with very thin slices of charcoal-grilled beef.

Makes 2 cups.

2 cloves garlic
1 onion, sliced
1 Tb. vegetable oil
1 pound white button mushrooms
3 to 10 serrano chiles, roasted, deveined, seeded, and cut in strips (see COOK'S NOTE)
8 tomatillos
½ tsp. cumin
Salt

COOK'S NOTE:

Use as many chiles as your taste and tolerance for heat dictates.

Fish Poached in Poblano Sauce

This is an unusual treatment of fish and is amenable to a wide range of garnishes, including shredded ginger, daikon or chopped cilantro.

6 poblano chiles
2 cloves garlic, peeled
½ onion, sliced
10 cilantro sprigs
1 Tb. light oil, such as soybean or corn
Salt
1 cup water
½ cup dry cheese, such as feta or dry Monterey Jack
6 fish fillets, such as red snapper or 6 fish steaks, such as halibut

Roast chiles and remove skins, seeds and veins. Liquify the roasted chiles, garlic cloves, onion, and cilantro in a blender or food processor.

Preheat oven to 350° F.

Heat oil in a frying pan and add the chile mixture. Cook over medium heat for 5 to 10 minutes. Do not brown. Add salt to taste, 1 cup of water and the cheese. Mix together. Arrange the fish fillets in an ovenproof casserole dish. Cover with the poblano sauce and bake in the preheated oven for 30 minutes or until fish is just done. Serve with rice.

Makes 6 servings.

Variation: Grill fish, then top with 2 to 3 tablespoons of poblano sauce.

Cooking with Dried Chiles

In this section tamales, adobos and cooking with dried chiles in general are covered. Tamale dough can be notoriously bland, and yet tamales can be one of the richest, most flavorful of Mexican or Mexican-inspired foods, especially when filled with well-seasoned meats. In part this is because dried chiles are used to cook many of the fillings which go into tamales, and because good cooks incorporate the broth from the meats into the masa or tamale dough. Adobos are thick pastes, somewhat sour, made with dried chiles and vinegar, plus any number of other ingredients. In the Philippines, adobos include soy sauce as well as vinegar and chiles and often are used with fish dishes. The technique involves combining dried chiles with garlic, perhaps tomato, some herbs and the new ingredient, vinegar. Adobo sauces are strong, and not every palate readily accepts them. If you wish to tone them down, add more water or broth at the last moment.

Using the many different dried chiles will expand your culinary repertoire tremendously. Dried chiles can be used whole; pureed with other ingredients as a paste for soups, stews and sauces; and ground into pure powders. (See the next section for grinding chiles). The powders can then be mixed to create further flavors. And the flavors will be subtle. Negro chile, dried and ground, mixed with the dried and ground ancho chile will create a rich blending of flavors which can be used in either a dominant or background role. Perhaps you have been to a Mexican restaurant touted by friends as "really authentic" and found that the enchiladas, burritos and tamales were unlike any you had ever tasted. Chances are you were eating meats and sauces built upon a mingling of flavors created by using dried chiles rather than fresh ones.

The best fresh chiles are seasonal. Their main period of production is from early summer to late fall. When chiles are plentiful, take some home and dry them. Not only will you have a store of chiles, you'll also have some which have quite different flavors than fresh chiles. (See page 21 for how to dry chiles at home.)

When shopping for dried chiles, look for ones that are still supple; they are the freshest of the large chiles. Small chiles such as the pequin and tepin dry very quickly, and they will be crisp. In choosing these, look for packets that have intact chiles; avoid those with lots of seeds at the bottom, indicating that many of the chiles are broken.

COOK'S NOTE:

The following is a list of dried chiles commonly found in supermarkets: arbol, California, New Mexico, ancho, mulato, negro, Colorado, japones, tepin and pequin.

Preparing Dried Chiles

Cleaning

Most dried chiles available in American markets have been dried and packed in the hot dusty areas of Mexico, so don't be dismayed when you open a package of chiles and see them covered with dust—this doesn't mean they are old. Just wipe the chiles off gently with a soft dry cloth.

Toasting

Most cooks experienced with dried chiles recommend toasting them before using them. This is done with a comal, dry griddle or cast-iron frying pan. Heat should be moderately hot and even. Press the chiles against the hot metal with the back of a wooden spoon, or with your hand. You will see the chiles begin to plump up and soften. They should NOT become crisp or undergo any color change. The toasting process takes only a few minutes.

Seeding and Deveining

A rule of thumb is to remove the seeds and veins from most of the large dried chiles such as the ancho, mulato and pasilla. From the small chiles such as the pequin, Thai and arbol, remove the seeds and veins to diminish the hotness; leave them in for the heat.

Removing the Skins

It is difficult to remove the skins from dried chiles, even after toasting and soaking. Many traditional cooks skip this time-consuming process. However, if you are particularly sensitive to bitterness, you may want to remove the skin. (Some people think the skins are a source of bitterness in dried chiles. Others are concerned with texture, as it is sometimes difficult to grind the skin into a smooth paste.)

Soaking

Often a recipe will call for soaking the chiles in either water or a broth before using. This process makes the chile easier to puree. Other times no soaking is required.

Pureeing

Many recipes will call for using the rough stone of the molcajete to puree or blend the dried chiles into a paste with peeled cloves of garlic and, sometimes, herbs and tomatoes. Purists swear that this technique creates a very special meld of flavors that can't be duplicated in a blender or food processor. However, few people have time to pursue this method, and the result from the machines may be slightly different, but is still delicious.

Adobo Pork with White Rice

This adobo is well suited to a hearty, simple occasion. Serve it with simply prepared white rice; you'll find plenty of flavor from the sauce.

In a molcajete, blender or food processor, combine all the ingredients except the pork. Process until you have a thick paste. Cook in a saucepan over a low heat for 10 to 15 minutes.

If you are using pork chops, brown them in a dry frying pan, then cover with the sauce and cook 35 to 45 minutes or until the pork is thoroughly cooked. If using a pork roast, rub first with salt, then roast in a 350° F. oven for 1½ hours. Remove from oven and cover with the adobo sauce. Return to oven and cook another 45 minutes.

Serve either dish with white boiled or steamed rice.

Makes 6 to 8 servings.

1 onion, peeled and sliced thin
3 cloves garlic, peeled
2 dried ancho chiles, toasted and seeded
1 negro chile, toasted and seeded
1 tomato, halved and toasted
½ cup distilled vinegar
½ cup chicken broth
1 tsp. salt
3- to 4-pound pork roast or 6 to 8 pork chops

Chuck Roast with Negro Chiles

*T*he thick, black sauce created from the negro chiles and then combined with the roast beef makes an earthy dish. Serve with oregano roasted potatoes or traditional flour tortillas. Leftovers (if there are any) make an excellent filling for tamales, enchiladas, rellenos or any sandwich.

2 negro chiles, toasted, seeded and soaked in 1 cup water for 30 minutes

4 cloves garlic, peeled

1 red bell pepper, roasted, peeled and seeded

1 tsp. ground cloves

1 cup beef consomme or beef broth

3-to 4-pound chuck roast

1 tsp. salt

Drain chiles. Combine with all ingredients except chuck roast and salt in a blender or food processor. Cook for 5 to 10 minutes over low heat. Reserve.

Preheat oven to 325° F.

Trim as much fat as possible from the roast. Rub with salt. In a heavy iron skillet or dutch oven sear both sides of the roast. The meat should be nicely browned. Drain off fat and cook in the preheated oven for 2 hours. Remove; drain the fat and juices. Baste the meat with all the negro chile sauce. Roast for another 45 minutes to 1 hour. The meat should be very tender and easily fall away from the bone.

Makes 6 servings.

VARIATION:

Grill your favorite steaks, then serve them with the sauce or baste the steaks with the sauce as they grill.

Making Tamales

It is in tamale making that the dried chiles really have a special place. Dried chiles are soaked in a flavored broth, which is then used to moisten the tamale dough. Often meats succulent with juices, chiles and peppercorns are shredded and used to fill the tamales. Many Americans think of tamales as corn husks spread with a dough made from cornmeal, but in fact there are many kinds of tamales.

In Mexico, for example, whatever leaves are local in a particular region are used to make tamales. In the Yucatan, abundant with tropical plants, banana and avocado leaves are the usual tamale wrappers, not corn husks. In Central Mexico "corundas" are the specialty — little spoonfuls of rich, vegetable-packed masa wrapped in sisal leaves and twisted into small crowns.

For the tamale dough, if possible, go to a Mexican delicatessen and order ready-made dough, called masa. It will be quite stiff, and you will need to add lard and broth, generally in these proportions: 1 pound lard and 1 cup broth for 10 pounds of dough. Adjust for salt.

If you cannot purchase masa, you can make your own. There are several packaged mixes available at most chain markets nationwide, Quaker brand among them.

Whether you buy ready-made dough or make your own, the principle of incorporating lard is the same—to beat air into the dough, making it light and fluffy.

For the tamale wrappers, dried corn husks are most commonly used. You can also prepare your own corn husks to use throughout the year. Trim the outer husks of fresh ears of corn, being careful not to shred them. Hang them up to dry on a clothesline. They will dry quickly on hot days. When they are a bleached yellow, take them down and store them in plastic or paper bags until ready to use. You may also freeze them.

When you are ready to use the store-bought or home-dried corn husks, soak them in hot water for 20 to 30 minutes to restore their supple texture. Dry them slightly with paper towels

COOK'S NOTE:

Lard, rather than vegetable shortening, is the time-honored ingredient for making the best tamales. Tamale specialists tell us that a properly prepared dough will be light, fluffy and most flavorful only when lard is used. If you wish to substitute a vegetable shortening, do so, but remember that flavor and texture will be altered.

Traditionally, the lard is whipped by hand until it is light and fluffy. Using your hand as a paddle, turn the lard over and over, beating air into it. The purpose here is to lighten the lard with air, consequently achieving light dough for the tamales. However, this method is practical only if you are making a large quantity of dough, 10 pounds or more. In making just enough dough for 3 dozen, we suggest using a food processor (see Basic Tamale Dough, page 47).

before using. They should not be wet when you spread the dough on them.

If you are using banana leaves, steam them for 2 to 3 minutes to soften the thick mid-rib.

Other suggestions for wrappers are: fresh, green corn husks (no soaking necessary); large leaves, such as chard, cabbage, greenleaf chicory or grape leaves. Each different wrapper will impart a different flavor to your tamales.

To spread the dough onto the wrapper, start at the bottom or small end of the husk or leaf and spread the dough just slightly off center. Use the back of a wooden spoon or a plastic spatula to spread the dough about ¼-inch thick. Use one to two tablespoons of filling per tamale. Don't spread the filling all the way to the edges of the wrapper. Especially at the stem or small end, leave 1-inch margins. That way, when the tamales are put in the steamer, even if the bottom of the tamale is in the water, the dough will not be.

To steam tamales, have ready a large steamer with a rack (1 gallon or larger). Add enough water to it so that the level reaches no higher than the base of the rack. To protect the tamales, place a layer of corn wrappers over the rack. Then place the tamales side by side, ends up. Bring water to low boil and hold.

Steam medium-size tamales for at least 40 minutes; check the water level at least every 15 minutes. Check one tamale at this point to make certain the masa is cooked (it falls away from the corn husk), and the filling is hot. Allow 50 to 60 minutes for large tamales.

Basic Tamale Dough

In the food processor, cream the lard. Alternately add the masa and the broth, continuing to process until the dough is smooth. Add the salt and blend in. The dough should have a spreadable texture, somewhat like cookie dough. It should not be runny, but neither should it be so stiff that it pulls away from the husk or leaf as you spread. Adjust texture with more broth if too thick, with masa harina if too thin. A really good tamale dough will float when a teaspoon of it is dropped into a glass of cold water. Try it.

Makes enough dough for 3 dozen tamales.

¾ cup lard
6 cups masa harina de maiz (packaged mix)
9 cups chicken, beef, or pork broth
1 tsp. salt

Roast Pork Tamales

C ooked shredded pork is one of the most typical—and most delicious—ingredients for meat tamales. These may be shaped into small slender tamales or large plump ones, depending upon your interests. Either way the combination of succulent roast pork and full-bodied dried chiles is hard to beat.

6 dried ancho or
  California chiles
1 cup broth from the
  roast pork
3 cloves garlic, peeled
½ onion
2 Tb. vegetable oil
Salt
2 cups cooked shredded
  roast pork
½ Basic Tamale Dough
  (see page 47)
12 to 15 tamale
  wrappers

Toast the chiles on a comal or in a hot frying pan until soft. Be careful not to burn. Remove and discard the seeds. Tear into pieces and soak for 10 minutes in the broth. Mash the garlic and onion, and place in a blender or food processor. Add the chiles. Blend until very smooth.

In a heavy saucepan heat the oil. Add the sauce from the blender. Add remaining broth if any. Stir and cook for 15 minutes. Season with salt to taste. Add the shredded meat to the sauce when it is still runny. Set aside.

Spread the dough onto the wrappers (see page 46). In the center of the spread dough, place a spoonful of pork filling. Fold the bottom of the tamale wrapper up over the filling. Then fold each side. Top remains open. Steam for 40 minutes.

Makes 12 to 15 large tamales.

COOK'S NOTE:

Some cooks tie each tamale with a string around the middle. If you are making several different types of tamales and steaming them all together, color code them by tying each type with a different colored string.

Corunda Tamales

These are the little steamed crowns made with fresh corn kernels and bits of roasted red and green peppers stirred into the masa. The taste here is very subtle and unusual, as each of the three corns used has a similar, yet distinct flavor. The trick with the corundas is tying. The long thin sisal leaves have a tablespoon full of masa placed about two-thirds of the way down the leaf, and then the dough is tied into the leaf just the way the latigo strap is wound around the cinch ring of a western saddle. We suggest practicing the tying technique a few times without the dough, just to get the idea. Also, the filling can be used with dried corn husks or other leaves (see pages 45–46) as wrappers.

Seed peppers and mince. Mince onion. Sauté peppers and onion in oil until just translucent. Cut corn kernels from ear with a sharp knife. Gently mix sautéed vegetables, corn, and ground chile in dough. Put the dough two-thirds of the way down the leaf and tie as illustrated below. Steam in a steamer basket for 20 minutes. It's best to have only one layer, if possible. If not, steam 5 to 8 minutes longer.

Makes 3 dozen.

2 paprika or pimiento peppers, roasted
1 green bell pepper, roasted
½ onion
1 Tb. corn or other light vegetable oil
1 ear fresh white corn
1 ear fresh yellow corn
1 tsp. ground ancho chile
Basic Tamale Dough (see page 47)
Sisal leaves

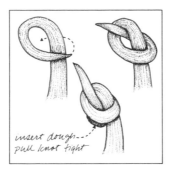

insert dough---
pull knot tight

Tamales with Huitlacoche

This recipe was created by Michael Roberts, chef at Trumps' Restaurant in Los Angeles. We arrived one day with a box of huitlacoche (corn fungus) for him to experiment with, and 20 minutes later this beautiful dish appeared at our table. The inky black of the huitlacoche sauce against the golden colors of the tamale is really striking. The taste is again corn but this time in four different states: ground, in the masa; yellow sweet corn; white sweet corn; and the corn fungus.

2 ears huitlacoche, removed from cob (about 1 cup)
¼ cup minced shallots
2 Tb. unsalted butter
½ cup dry white wine
1 Tb. heavy cream
2 dozen corn husks
Corunda Tamale dough (see page 49)

Cut the huitlacoche into large chunks. Don't worry about the black powdery spores spilling out as you cut. You'll still have plenty. Sauté the shallots in the butter. Add the chopped huitlacoche. Simmer over a low heat for 15 minutes. Increase heat to high; add wine. Continue to cook until sauce is reduced by half. Reduce heat. Stir in cream.

Meanwhile, spread corn husks with the dough and steam them for 20 minutes.

To serve, open the tamale husks to show the colorful filling. Spoon the huitlacoche sauce over the open end of the tamale.

Makes 2 dozen.

BUYER'S NOTE:

Look for huitlacoche at farmers' markets and at pick-your-own corn farms. Tell the farmer what you are looking for and describe it. You may need to specially request the huitlacoche.

Tamales with Peanuts

Leftover tamales from this recipe are delicious when removed from the husk, deep-fried, and served with sour cream. Of course, the original tamales are wonderful too!

Prepare masa, mixing in water and lard alternately. Set aside. Soften the corn husks in hot water and set aside.

Boil the ancho and cascabel chiles, the garlic and onion in 2 cups water until chiles are soft. Drain, reserving the cooking water. Puree the chile mixture, adding a little reserved water as needed to form a medium-thick paste. Empty this paste into a bowl. Process the shelled peanuts in blender or food processor until they form a *crunchy*, not smooth peanut butter. Mix into the chile puree.

To form tamales, pat out the dough to a ¼-inch thick layer onto a clean damp dishcloth. Spread the peanut-chile butter mixture over the masa to within 1 inch of edges. Now, slowly roll up the dough, jelly roll fashion, making 3 to 4 "folds." When you have a complete roll, cut thin slices off the roll. You will have many little pinwheel circles of masa and filling. Place each slice in the center of a corn husk, fold as in Corunda tamales (see page 49). Put in a steamer and steam for about 45 minutes to 1 hour. Tamales are cooked when the masa does not stick to the husk.

Makes 24 medium tamales.

3½ cups masa harina
2 cups water
½ cup lard
3 to 4 dozen dried corn husks
3 ancho chiles, seeded
3 cascabel chiles, seeded
3 cloves garlic
¼ onion
1¼ cups freshly roasted peanuts, shelled (or crunchy natural peanut butter)

Chilean Tamales

Called humitas *in Chile, these unusual tamales contain either sweet or spicy fillings. Half of ours is sweet; the other half is spicy.*

12 ears tender corn (save husks and cobs)

1 onion

3 Tb. lard or vegetable oil

Salt

3 Tb. chopped fresh basil

3 serrano chiles, seeded and finely chopped

2 Tb. sugar

Husk ears of corn; soften largest husks in hot water. Finely chop onion and sauté in lard. Grate kernels from cobs and add to skillet with salt to taste and basil. Divide corn mixture into 2 parts. Add serranos to one part, sugar to the other.

Place a tablespoon of corn mixture on each husk, fold over, and tie. (It is helpful to use different knots or folds to distinguish hot from sweet fillings, or use colored strings as described in COOK'S NOTE on page 48.) Cover bottom of large pot with corncobs. Cover with boiling salted water, lay *humitas* on top of cobs, cover tightly and steam about 40 minutes.

Serves 6 to 8.

Ancho Salsa

We've used this thick, rich ancho salsa in composed salads, thinning the salsa with a light oil to create a salad dressing texture. Rocket, Feta Cheese, Tomatillos and Avocados with Ancho Dressing (page 92) is a good example of an unusual way to use this salsa. More traditionally, use it with any filled dish, such as burritos or enchiladas.

Toast anchos on a comal or griddle until soft. Remove seeds and veins. Put in a blender or food processor with the cilantro and process until almost a paste. Add a tablespoon of hot water if necessary. Cut tomato into quarters and tomatillos into halves and toast skin side on comal or griddle for 2 to 3 minutes, just long enough to slightly sear. Add to the processor along with the pumpkin seeds, if you choose to use them. They will act as a thickener, and also give an additional flavor. Process all the ingredients until very smooth. Add salt to taste. To thin, add a little oil until you reach the desired consistency.

Makes 1 cup.

3 dried ancho chiles
3 Tb. cilantro leaves
1 large red tomato
3 tomatillos
1 Tb. pumpkin seeds
   (optional)
Salt
Peanut or safflower oil

Chile Pesto

The basil and chile combination here makes it difficult to sort Italian from Mexican, but the resulting meld of flavors is delicious, regardless of ethnic origins. Use to top pasta, rice or polenta, even burritos.

2 dried Colorado chiles
1 dried cascabel chile
1 cup boiling water
1 clove garlic, peeled
½ inch fresh ginger, peeled
2 Tb. onion, minced
1 Tb. chopped parsley
1 large leaf fresh basil
½ tsp. salt
1 cup chicken broth
1½ Tb. corn oil
Pepitos, for topping

Toast the dried chiles on a comal or griddle. Let cool; slit; remove seeds and tear into pieces. Place in blender. Put boiling water over the pieces and let stand for at least 10 minutes. Add garlic, ginger, 1 tablespoon onion, parsley and basil to the chile-water mixture. (Reserve the rest of the onion for sautéeing.) Blend all until very smooth. Add salt and broth. Blend again.

Heat oil in heavy saucepan. Add remaining tablespoon of onion and sauté until transparent. Add the chile mixture. Stir and simmer over low heat for 10 to 15 minutes. Top with pepitos.

Makes 2 cups.

Whole Baby Bok Choy with Hot Chile Chips

This is a good dish to satisfy a craving for potato chips!

Steam baby bok choy until just tender, about 8 minutes.

Preheat oven to 400° F.

Peel and slice potatoes into ¼-inch widths. Place them in a single layer on an oiled baking sheet and bake for 10 minutes on the first side. Turn. Bake another 8 minutes. They should be firm, but not crispy brown. Remove.

Mix chile powder and salt, and dust on potatoes. Heat 2 tablespoons oil in a wok. When very hot, add the chile-dusted potatoes and the pequins, and stir constantly until thoroughly crisp. Remove and keep hot. Put bok choy into same wok and continue to stir until it is thoroughly coated and hot. Return chile chips to wok and serve.

Makes 4 servings.

4 baby green bok choy
2 large baking potatoes
1 Tb. ancho chile powder (see pages 61–62)
1 tsp. salt
Vegetable oil
3 pequin chiles, crumbled

Grilled Steak Slivers in Chipotle Peanut Sauce

This dish has some of the fiery flavors of southeast Asian cooking and is great accompanied with Asian beer.

4 cloves garlic, sliced

1 onion, sliced

1 Tb. vegetable oil

2 large, very ripe tomatoes

4 canned chipotles, reserving sauce

½ cup unsalted peanuts

½ cup beef broth

Salt

1 pound beef top round, very thinly sliced

1 lime

Prepare a charcoal grill.

Cook the garlic cloves and the onion slices in the oil until translucent. Puree the tomatoes, the chipotles and the peanuts with broth in a blender or food processor. Add the mixture to the onion and garlic and cook for 5 to 10 minutes. Add a tablespoon or more of the sauce from the canned chipotles if you wish more heat. Salt to taste. Rub the sliced meat lightly with juice from half the lime and grill over very high heat a few seconds on each side, just enough to heat and char the meat. Serve with a spoonful of the sauce accompanied by a lime slice. Plain white rice is a good accompaniment.

Makes 4 servings.

Hot and Spicy Lentils

This dish makes a nice alternative to the usual pinto bean chile dishes.

Follow instructions on package for cooking lentils, and add the Fresno chiles. When lentils are just tender, pour off all but ¾ cup liquid. Set aside.

Toast, devein and seed the ancho chiles, then soak them for 20 minutes in just enough water to cover them. Quarter the tomato and liquify it in a blender or food processor with the anchos, the water they soaked in, the onion, garlic and oregano. Cook the mixture in the oil for 3 or 4 minutes. Chop the sweet peppers into small pieces and add to the mixture. Cook another 3 or 4 minutes, then add the mixture to the lentils. Simmer slowly for 30 to 40 minutes. Add salt to taste and serve with corn tortillas.

Makes 6 servings.

1¼ cups dry lentils
3 Fresno chiles
4 dried ancho chiles
1 tomato
½ onion
1 clove garlic
1 Tb. fresh oregano leaves or 1 tsp. dry
1 Tb. peanut or other light oil
2 sweet red peppers or 1 yellow and 1 red
Salt
Corn tortillas

Black Shrimp and Jicama Appetizer

*S*ubtle *tastes and textures make an unusual mix in this striking dish.*

4 dried negro chiles
½ cup tequila
1 jicama
1 lime
2 cloves garlic, peeled and mashed
1 avocado
4 Tb. sour cream, crème fraîche or Mexican crema
½ pound shrimp, cooked and deveined
Ancho chile powder (see pages 61–62)
Freshly ground black pepper

Toast, devein and seed the chiles and soak them in the tequila. Wash and peel the jicama, then cut it into ½-inch cubes. Sprinkle with lime juice to prevent discoloring.

In a blender or food processor, liquify the garlic cloves and the chile-tequila mixture. Peel the avocado, discard the pit and cut into ½-inch cubes. Sprinkle with lime juice to prevent discoloration. Mix the chile-tequila mixture with the sour cream. Combine the shrimp, jicama and avocado, then add the sour cream mixture, tossing gently. Serve topped with ancho chile powder and freshly ground black pepper.

Makes 6 servings.

Clams-in-Their-Shells Soup

An extremely satisfying dish, reminiscent of cioppino, *the classic Italian seafood stew.*

When you buy the clams (or dig them), make sure you take only those which are tightly closed. Soak the clams in a basin or bucket of cold water to get them to disgorge themselves of sand if they are freshly dug. If store bought, a good rinsing under running water is usually adequate.

Open the dried chiles, remove the seeds and veins and soak them for 10 minutes in just enough hot water to cover them. Put the chiles and the water in the blender with the onion, red bell peppers and garlic; liquify.

Wash potatoes and cut into 1-inch pieces. Cut squash into ½-inch-thick slices. Set aside.

In a large soup pot, cook the chile mixture in the oil for 3 to 5 minutes. Add the water, squash, potatoes, spinach, broccoli, and epazote. When the vegetables are done, add clams and cook 3 minutes or just until the shells open. Add salt and pepper to taste and serve hot with slices of lemon.

Makes 4 to 6 servings.

2 to 2½ pounds fresh clams, in their shells

2 dried ancho chiles

2 dried arbol chiles

1 slice onion

4 large red bell peppers, seeded and coarsely chopped

3 garlic cloves, peeled and chopped

4 new potatoes

4 zucchini squash, 2 yellow and 2 green if possible

1 Tb. vegetable oil

6 cups water

1 bunch fresh spinach

1 cup broccoli florets

2 branches epazote (thyme can be substituted, but flavor of soup will be very different)

Salt and freshly ground black pepper

1 lemon, sliced

Sweet Chipotles

These make a deliciously different accompaniment for curries and pilafs. Try pureeing them to use as a sandwich spread with roast duck or venison, as the strong flavors go well together.

1 can (6¾ ounces)
 chipotle chiles
1 head garlic, cloves
 peeled
½ tsp. whole cloves
1 cinnamon stick
4 thick orange slices,
 with rind
2 cups water
½ cup white vinegar
2 Tb. brown sugar
Salt
Peanut oil

Cook all the ingredients except the oil for 10 minutes over medium-low heat. Remove the mixture to a large glass jar with a cover. Pack loosely. Cover with ¼-inch layer of oil and let cool. Cover with the lid and refrigerate. They will keep for up to 3 weeks in the refrigerator.

Makes 2 cups.

Ancho Vinegar-Herb Rellenos

This is an unusual relleno in that it uses dried, not fresh, chiles. The taste is rich and smoky.

4 dried ancho chiles
½ cup cider or white
 vinegar
2 branches fresh
 oregano
4 leaves fresh sage
2 branches fresh thyme
4 slices Monterey jack
 cheese
½ onion, peeled and
 chopped
Relleno batter (see page
 31)
Vegetable oil, for frying
Ancho Salsa (see page
 53)

Toast, seed and devein chiles. Combine vinegar and herbs in a saucepan; bring to a boil. Reduce heat and simmer for 10 minutes. Add anchos and let stand off the heat 10 minutes.

Put a slice of cheese and one-fourth the chopped onion into each chile. Dip filled chiles in relleno batter and fry in ½ inch oil until batter is browned and puffy. Serve with Ancho Salsa.

Makes 4 servings.

Cooking with Chile Powders and Salts

Dried chiles ground into powders are relatively foreign to most American cooks, who are used to buying prepared chile powders that contain any number of spices and seasonings blended together. Common ingredients are cumin, oregano, allspice, onion and garlic, as well as the chiles and salt.

In Mexico simple chile powders are abundant and used at times with what we might consider a heavy hand. But the results are interesting. True chile flavors are distinct from other seasonings and lend to fruits, vegetables and meats an earthy piquancy unmatched by black pepper or American-style commercial chile powder. To give you an idea of just how much the powdered chiles are used, picture a busy street in Mexico lined with vendors selling grilled and steamed corn, sliced jicama and fruit cups. Each one of these will have powdered chile to be added at the end when the customer is served. Cool, frothy beer is also topped with chile powder, lime and salt. Snack foods have chile coated on them, too. Taco chips, fava beans and peanuts are among a few flavored with chile.

Powdered chiles are effectively used in bean dishes, stews, cream sauces, salad dressings and soups. It takes practice to determine just how much powdered chile you like, just as it does to approximate yield from whole dried chiles. A rough guideline is that one tablespoon of chile powder made from large chiles, such as ancho or California, is equal to one large pod. One tablespoon prepared from the smaller types, such as the arbol, Thai or even cascabel, represents three or four chiles.

Some cooks remove the seeds of the dried chiles before grinding them because the seeds are bitter. Other cooks don't bother. Our suggestion is to remove seeds from the large chiles, not from the small ones. There is not much left of a small, thin-skinned chile, such as the arbol, after you've removed its seeds. If you need to reduce the heat of a chile powder, do remove the seeds, as some of the hotness is stored within the seeds.

Almost all the dried chiles may be ground and used as powders, either pure or mixed with salt. Grind the dried chiles you like, then experiment. The mild California adds a light, pungent taste; the ancho gives an earthier flavor; the Colorado or arbol will add heat. Remember that the ground product will reflect the same characteristics as the dried form. The amount of salt to blend with the ground chiles depends upon the specific recipe and personal taste.

Grinding Dried Chiles

The traditional method of preparing a chile powder is by grinding the chiles in a molcajete. Not only is this very time consuming, but it is also dangerous to the novice—you can expect fume and fine chile dust to aggravate your eyes, nose and mouth as well as your hands. It is far better to use a grinder or a blender for making powders. An inexpensive coffee grinder is ideal—you might even want to buy one just for grinding chiles. A blender works just fine too. You may wish to grind enough for a small supply to have on hand. Store it just as you would whole dried chiles, in a sealed container away from the direct light.

In Jalisco, Mexico, dried chiles are ground and blended with other seasonings and moistened to make a salty paste called *birria*, which is used to coat and flavor meat as it slowly cooks. The baked meats made this way are unduplicated in flavor. Thickly spread with the paste, a roast is placed in a heavy cooking pot, covered tightly and slowly cooked—in some cases wrapped in leaves and lowered into a pit full of hot coals for slow, direct cooking. Pork, goat, lamb or beef may be used, or combinations of the meats. Typical cuts are joints, legs, shoulder and even pieces of neck meat.

Jicama Appetizer

*T*he white sweet, succulent tuber, jicama, is frequently eaten alone with just a few condiments such as minced onion, grated cheese, lime juice and chile powder sprinkled on top of a cross-sectional slice. It is excellent combined with citrus. Here we have mixed oranges with jicama as a simple starter. You could also use it as a salad or fruit dessert, depending upon the occasion.

Prepare the ingredients. Mix together in a bowl the jicama, orange slices, lime juice, salt and mint leaves. Spoon into individual serving bowls. Sprinkle with a bit of chile powder.
   Makes 6 to 8 servings.

3 cups sliced jicama, cut into bite-size pieces
2 cups oranges, peeled, membranes removed and sliced
Juice of two limes
¼ tsp. salt (optional)
2 tsp. mint leaves, chopped or shredded
Dash of chile pequin powder

Jalapeno-Ham Sandwiches

*A*nother starter or lunch feature are open-face sandwiches which are broiled just before serving. Cut them into small triangular wedges if you wish a small sandwich; otherwise keep them large to hold the jalapeno strips.

Roast the jalapenos. Peel, remove the seeds, and slice into thin strips. Spread each slice of bread with mayonnaise and mustard. Place one piece of ham, one piece of cheese and jalapeno strips on the bread. Sprinkle with chile powder. Place on cookie sheet and put under a preheated broiler for 2 to 3 minutes, until the cheese bubbles and melts.
   Makes 4 open-face sandwiches.

4 jalapenos
4 bread slices
Mayonnaise
Dijon mustard
4 slices ham
4 slices Monterey Jack cheese
Powdered colorado chile

Grilled Corn on the Cob

C orn cooked in this manner is delicious and colorful with white crème fraîche and red ground chile slathered over the ears. This recipe uses corn that is slightly overripe. Make the crème fraîche one day in advance (see page 23), and grind the chiles ahead of time, too.

4 ears starchy, slightly
   overripe corn
¾ cup crème fraîche
¼ cup finely chopped
   onions
¼ cup dry jack cheese,
   finely grated (queso
   anejo or Romano will
   also work well)
Sea salt
2 Tb. freshly ground
   ancho chile powder

Have ready a medium hot grill. Prepare the ears of corn by opening the shucks and pulling off the silks while leaving the shucks intact. After you have removed the silks, return the shucks to their normal position. If they are dry, dampen them. Grill for 10 minutes or so — the timing depends upon the size of the ears. Do not overcook or allow the starchy kernels to become hard.

Once off the grill, remove the shucks. Spread an ample amount of crème fraîche over each ear. Sprinkle with the onion, cheese, a bit of salt to taste and a dash of chile powder.

Makes 4 servings.

Birria Baked Meat

We learned about birria from a friend who brought the dried seasonings back to California: a blend of ground chiles, oregano, garlic, cumin and lots of coarsely ground salt. With her help we have devised a mixture that is a very good substitute for the authentic one. This recipe uses a dry birria rather than a paste.

Mix the two chile powders together. Mash the chopped onion and garlic into the chile powders. Strip the leaves from the oregano and chop finely. Grind the cumin and allspice in a mortar and pestle. Place all the ingredients in a shallow pan and mix with the tines of a fork or with your fingers. Dry on a cookie sheet at the lowest setting of your oven, stirring occasionally for 4 to 6 hours.

Preheat oven to 325° F.

Trim away excess fat from meat. Pat the chile mixture onto the surface of the meat, pressing it in with your hand. Completely cover the meat with the chile. Place the meat on a shallow pan or in a dutch oven, cover and seal. Bake it very slowly in the preheated oven for 2½ hours. Meat will fall away from the bone and should be a very dark brown. Serve with warm corn tortillas and El Rancho Beans.

Makes 6 to 8 servings.

3 dried ancho chiles, ground into powder

2 dried cascabel chiles, ground into powder (Substitute guajillo chiles if necessary)

1 Tb. onion, finely chopped

3 cloves garlic, finely minced

1 large sprig fresh oregano, 6 inches long

1 tsp. cumin seed

5 allspice cloves

1 Tb. sea salt (this amount may be reduced)

4- to 5-pound chuck roast or pork loin roast

Corn tortillas

El Rancho Beans (see page 68)

Fresh Tomato-Chile Soup

This soup is very nice at room temperature, or it may be reheated and ladled steaming hot into bowls. Serve it simply, but be sure to include several garnishes.

8 medium to large very ripe tomatoes

1 large clove garlic, minced

¼ tsp. hot chile powder, made from Colorado, Thai or arbol chiles

Chopped green onions

Chopped cilantro

Crushed cumin seed

Wedges of fresh lime

Sea salt

Tortilla chips

Wash the tomatoes, but do not core. Place in broiler pan and broil until the skins are brown and shrivelled and the interior is soft.

Put the tomatoes through a food mill or puree in a blender. Make a puree. If necessary use a sieve to remove any bits of skin. Add the garlic and chile powder.

Garnish with the green onions, cilantro, cumin seed, lime wedges and salt; serve with tortilla chips.

Makes 4 servings.

Using Hot Chiles with Beans

In their simplest form beans are simmered until their skins and pulp are soft. In a few words (entire books are written just about beans) we wish to give you some cooking hints.

1. Always use fresh beans if you have a choice. Their flavor is better and they cook more rapidly than older ones.

2. Always sort and wash beans. Even with our efficient packaging methods, pebbles the size of beans are easily missed in the sorting methods.

3. You do not need to soak beans before cooking them. You will need to cook beans for several hours.

4. Never add other ingredients to the first stage of cooking. Simmer the beans in water by themselves until they are almost tender.

5. Add the flavoring ingredients, such as epazote or chiles, for the last hour of cooking.

6. Serve the beans the following day if possible. They will taste much better.

7. If you wish to make refried beans, mash the beans to a pulp. Add a bit of lard or oil to a skillet, heat and add the bean pulp. Cook and turn the beans as they "refry."

El Rancho Beans

*Y*ou may use pintos or other beans in this recipe. There are so many variations and so many favorites that we don't really expect you to follow this recipe exactly. But these are very good and a favorite of ours.

2 cups small red beans, sorted and rinsed

1 ½ quarts cold water

1 ham hock

3 cloves garlic, coarsely chopped

1 onion, quartered and the quarters sliced

1 tsp. chile powder, made from a mixture of ancho and arbol

1 tsp. cumin seeds, crushed

2 tsp. salt

Cook the beans in the water, adding more water if necessary over the period, for 3 to 4 hours at a low simmer. When you can easily smash a bean between your thumb and forefinger, add the ham hock, garlic, onion, chile powder and cumin. Cook for another hour or so, until the meat on the ham hock begins to separate from the joint. At this point taste the beans, and season with salt. Make other seasoning adjustments. Remember that as the beans stand their flavor improves.

Serves 10 small servings or 6 for healthy appetites.

Tinga Salad

Mexican meat salad with pickled chipotles makes a nice summer dish.

Shred pork and fry in lard until golden. Remove and drain. Season with a little vinegar from the chipotles. Wash and dry the lettuce. Arrange in an open salad bowl or on a platter. Place the meat and sliced chipotles on the lettuce. Sprinkle with crumbled cheese and add the sliced avocados and onion. Serve topped with the sour cream and negro chile powder.

    Makes 6 servings.

1 to 1¼ pounds cooked pork (leftover Birria Baked Meat is ideal)

4 ounces lard or vegetable oil

3 pickled chipotles, cut into slices and vinegar reserved

1 head iceberg or romaine lettuce

¼ pound fresh cheese, such as queso fresco or feta

3 avocados, peeled and sliced

1 red onion, sliced

2 Tb. sour cream or crème fraîche

2 Tb. negro chile powder

Mixed Grill with Chile Salts

Many vegetables as well as meats lend themselves to grill-ing. The addition of a mixture of ground chiles and salt before grilling adds another dimension of taste. It is fun to experiment with different woods, investigating what flavors they impart to the food. Try almond, grape and apple woods as well as the southwestern mesquite.

1 large eggplant
2 bunches scallions
2 green zucchini
2 yellow zucchini
3 large red onions
4 to 8 shiitake or cèpe
   mushrooms
1 pound lean lamb,
   cubed
Olive oil
1 Tb. negro chile
   powder
1 Tb. Chimayo powder
   (if available)
1 Tb. ancho chile
   powder
2 tsp. minced fresh
   oregano
½ tsp. salt or to taste
1 Tb. coarsely ground
   black pepper
Goat Cheese Cream
   (recipe follows)
Chopped cilantro
Dry jack or feta cheese,
   crumbled
8 sun-dried tomatoes,
   pureed

Slice the eggplant into pieces ½-inch thick. Slit the scallions lengthwise, but leave intact. Halve the zucchini lengthwise. Slice the red onions into pieces ½-inch thick. Halve the mushrooms lengthwise. Rub the vegetables and the lamb with olive oil. Thread the lamb on skewers. Mix the ground chiles, oregano, salt and pepper together. Rub the vegetables and the meat with the mixture. Grill and serve very hot, with side dishes of Goat Cheese Cream, chopped cilantro, dry crumbled cheese, and the puree of sun-dried tomatoes.

Makes 4 to 6 servings.

GOAT CHEESE CREAM

A delicious addition to any sandwich and a good topping for grilled or baked vegetables such as potatoes or onions.

Combine the goat cheese and the crème fraîche together to make a creamy mixture that will almost, but not quite, run from the spoon. Taste and add salt if desired.

Makes 1 cup.

4 ounces fresh goat cheese, such as Montrachet
½ cup crème fraîche
Salt, if necessary

Char-Baked Whole Onions

W*e first had this dish near Asti in northern Italy. The onions were caramelized in their own sugar and were exceptionally sweet. In Italy it was possible to buy them already cooked in the local markets. Later at a friend's house we were served a Yucatan version. Our recipe is a combination of the two. The taste of the dish will vary somewhat, depending upon the sweetness of the onions used. They are delicious rolled on a steamed corn tortilla.*

Preheat oven to 300° F. Rub unpeeled onions all over with olive oil and place them in a shallow dish 1 inch apart. Over them, pour chicken broth, which should cover them no more than halfway. Bake, uncovered, for 1 to 1½ hours. Slow cooking releases the natural sugars and allows the broth to be absorbed.

To serve, cut the onion in quarters, but only to within 1 inch of the bottom. Then, open the centers, pulling apart somewhat the onion layers, and divide the cheese and the chile powder mixture evenly among the onions.

Makes 6 servings.

3 medium onions, unpeeled (Maui, Vidalia or Parma for maximum sweetness)
1½ Tb. olive oil
1 cup chicken broth
½ pound fresh goat cheese
1 tsp. each negro chile powder and mulato chile powder, mixed together with salt as desired

Layered Quesadilla

*T*he combination of cool queso fresco, salty ham and hot, smoky chipotles gives this simple-to-make appetizer a mysterious flavor.

2 avocados
1 lime
Salt
12 slices ham
12 slices (4 by 4 by ¼-inch) Mexican fresh cheese (queso fresco) or farmer cheese
6 chipotle chiles, slivered
24 flour tortillas
6 dried arbol chiles, seeded and ground into powder

Peel and mash avocados; add lime juice to prevent discoloration. Salt to taste. Set aside.

Prepare sandwiches: place a slice of ham and cheese and a few slivers of chipotle on a tortilla. Cover with another tortilla. Heat the sandwich on both sides on a comal or griddle over low heat until cheese melts. Cut into quarters.

Place a spoonful of avocado topping on each sandwich section. Top with powdered arbol chile to taste. Repeat with remaining ingredients.

Makes 48 appetizers.

Garbanzo Quesadillas

These tasty quesadillas are delicious and are attractively served on a bed of leaf lettuce.

Prepare masa for tortillas as per package instructions. Soak, cook and peel garbanzos according to package directions. Puree garbanzos in the blender. Devein chiles, soak them in hot water, then puree. Mix the pureed garbanzos and chiles with the masa. Add salt and pepper to taste.

To form small tortillas, place 1 tablespoon cheese in center of each tortilla; fold them in half and seal edges well. Fry the quesadillas in enough oil to coat the pan over medium-high heat until they are golden brown. Blot on an absorbent towel. Spoon some sour cream on quesadillas and sprinkle with freshly ground ancho chile powder.

Makes 12 small quesadillas.

2 cups masa harina
1 cup dry garbanzos
  (see **COOK'S NOTE**)
2 ancho chiles
Salt and freshly ground
  black pepper
1 cup jack cheese,
  grated
Vegetable oil or lard,
  for frying
1 cup sour cream
4 dried ancho chiles
  ground into powder

COOK'S NOTE

Packaged humus may be substituted for cooked garbanzos.

Red Snapper with Achiote

*R*ed snapper is readily found in markets of both Mexico and the United States. It is popularly served with a tomato sauce enhanced by plenty of garlic and fresh herbs. In Mexico, jalapenos are frequently added to the fish sauce as well. In this particular recipe achiote paste—the blend of the ground annatto seed, ground chiles and other seasonings—is softened and rubbed on the fish fillets before cooking. They are then baked in a fresh tomato sauce and served with steaming rice. Substitute harissa (recipe follows) for achiote if you can't find achiote at a Hispanic grocery, but the flavors will be different.

2 fillets of red snapper, about 1 pound total
1 Tb. achiote paste
¼ cup boiling water
3 cloves garlic
½ onion
2 Tb. olive oil
2 to 3 tomatoes
1 yellow bell pepper
1 sprig oregano or 1 tsp. dried oregano
6 green olives
4 lime slices

Wash and pat dry the fish fillets; set aside.

Soften the achiote paste by combining with boiling water. (If you use harissa, use ⅛ cup water.) Blend until smooth. Spread the mixture on all sides of the fillets. Let stand for 10 minutes. Peel and mince the garlic. Chop the onion. Place oil in a skillet and sauté the garlic and onion. Add one fillet and briefly cook each side. Repeat with remaining fillet; remove to a baking dish.

Preheat oven to 325° F.

Peel, seed, and chop the tomatoes. Roast, peel and seed the pepper; cut into 1-inch slices. Add to the fish. Sprinkle the oregano leaves over the fish and cover. Bake in preheated oven for 25 minutes.

To serve, garnish with green olives and sliced lime. Serve with plain or seasoned rice.

Makes 3 to 4 servings.

HARISSA

3 ounces japones chiles
1 Tb. ground cumin
2 to 3 garlic cloves
¾ tsp. salt
¾ to 1 cup olive oil

Whir the chiles in a blender until they are coarsely ground. Add the cumin, garlic, salt, and enough olive oil to make a puree. (Do not overblend; the peppers should still be in small pieces.) Remove from the blender and mix in the remaining olive oil; adjust seasoning as desired.

Makes about 1 cup.

Making Moles and Pipians

Mole—the term conjures up images of the thick, dark, rich sauce from Mexico tasting of chocolate and spices. Derived from an old Nahuatl or Aztec word meaning "concoction," mole is more than one paricular sauce. You can find any number of kinds of moles just as you can enchiladas. Moles vary from region to region and perhaps more importantly, from household to household. You can make green mole with romaine lettuce, a tan mole with almonds and cascabel, a ruddy brown mole with ancho and Anaheims, and of course the almost black mole made with chocolate and mulatos. Fowl is one of the key ingredients, but pork and cooked vegetables are common as well.

There are many versions of how moles originated. The general lore is that an important visitor arrived at a convent in the city of Puebla de Los Angeles. Some say he was unexpected and that the cooks in the kitchen were taken off guard as they had few main supplies that day. However, they always had cooked turkey (it was wild in the area), chiles and, of course, chocolate. Rallying to serve this important man at least a full meal, one cook (some call her an angel, others a nun) began to make a spicy concoction of many ingredients. It was a huge success when served, and mole (molli in those days) was created.

Pipians are very similar to moles. Both may employ ground seeds and nuts as well as chiles, fowl and other seasonings. Pipians generally use larger quantities of nuts and seeds and are thicker than moles. Pipian recipes do not contain chocolate, but then, neither does Mole Verde. Pipians are also supposed to contain fewer total ingredients than moles, but when we ask our friends "just how many for each," they shrug their shoulders.

The joy of moles and pipians is the blending of ingredients. Each ingredient must be in balance or harmony with the others, and must never overshadow the whole. The rather strong chocolate-flavored moles in particular must be made with careful attention to ingredients and proportions, using peanuts, chiles, pumpkin seeds, allspice, cinnamon and some kind of fowl or vegetable. Typically moles will have more than one kind of chile: anchos, mulatos, chipotles. Both fresh and dried chiles are used.

Mole Negro de Oaxaca

Cook *the fowl of your choice, usually turkey for special occasions. Reserve broth for making mole.*

This dark mole requires negro chiles, mulatos, and/or anchos. A good proportion is 6 negro chiles and 4 mulatos. Toast the chiles. If you like an especially strong flavored mole, allow the skins to burn slightly.

Toast chiles, then seed, tear, and soak in the usual fashion (see pages 41–42). Set aside.

Fry the almonds, peanuts, and sesame seeds in the oil for 5 minutes. Drain oil and blend nuts and seeds in a food processor along with all ingredients except bread crumbs, arbol or serrano chile and fowl. Place the smoothly blended mixture into a deep saucepan and cook very slowly for 30 to 40 minutes or until it tastes done. (If mixture is too runny, add white bread crumbs.) Adjust seasonings. If it needs more piquant flavor, add a chile de arbol or serrano. Cut fowl into pieces and heat. Serve fowl on a platter with mole sauce poured over it and accompanied with Seasoned Rice.

Makes 6 servings.

6 negro chiles
4 mulato chiles
¼ cup almonds
1½ Tb. raw peanuts
1 Tb. sesame seeds
1 Tb. vegetable oil
2 tsp. oregano leaves
4 black peppercorns
1 clove
1 Tb. seedless raisins
1 avocado
2 ounces grated
    Mexican chocolate
4 tomatoes, chopped
1 tsp. salt
1 stale tortilla, torn in
    strips
3 cups broth, from
    cooked fowl
White bread crumbs, as
    needed
Arbol or serrano chile,
    optional
1 whole chicken, or
    turkey half, cooked
Seasoned Rice (see page
    79)

Mole Verde

1 chicken
½ onion
1 tsp. black pepper
1-inch cube fresh ginger
½ tsp. salt
4 Anaheim chiles
2 serrano chiles
4 tomatillos
1 Tb. pumpkin seeds
2 tsp. sesame seeds
8 almonds, blanched
2 Tb. vegetable oil
2 cloves garlic, peeled
½ yellow onion, peeled
1 green bell pepper
1 Tb. unsalted peanut
  butter
2 allspice cloves
1 tomato, chopped and
  seeded
1 cup chopped parsley
1 large head romaine
  lettuce
1 corn tortilla
Salt

*M*ole verde acquires its beautiful, rich, bright green color from romaine lettuce and Anaheim chiles. It is an excellent* pièce de résistance *for a dinner party. Serve with steaming hot corn tortillas and seasoned rice.*

Cut chicken into pieces and simmer slowly in enough water to cover the chicken. If you wish, season with onion, black pepper, ginger and salt. Set aside. Reserve 3 cups broth.

Roast the fresh chiles and skin. Seed and chop them. Toast the tomatillos. Blend chiles and tomatillos with one cup of the reserved broth. Set aside to season for 15 minutes.

Sauté the seeds and nuts in the oil. Puree in blender or food processor with chile mixture, garlic, onion, bell pepper, peanut butter, allspice and tomato. Add 1 cup broth. Next add the parsley and the lettuce and blend. Mixture should be bright green. If it is too watery, add the corn tortilla and blend again. You should use a total of 2 to 3 cups broth, but ingredients vary, and you may have to adjust.

Place the liquid in a saucepan and cook for 10 to 15 minutes, until the color changes to a darker green. Add salt to taste.

Meanwhile, heat the chicken in an ovenproof dish in a 350° F oven or in a microwave. Place it in a deep serving dish and pour the mole sauce over the chicken.

Makes 10 servings.

SEASONED RICE

There are many variations of seasoned rice. We like this one with the intense yellow that results from using elote.

Heat a heavy saucepan. Add the rice and oil. Stir constantly over medium-low heat until the rice is golden brown.

Drain off any remaining oil. Add the onion, tomato, garlic, cilantro, elote and salt. Stir for 30 seconds. Add the liquid. Stir and simmer for one minute, then cover and steam for 18 to 20 minutes. At the very end of the cooking period take off lid for final drying. Fluff rice with fork just before serving.

Makes 4 to 6 servings.

1 cup white rice
¼ cup vegetable oil
1 Tb. chopped onion
½ cup chopped tomato
1 tsp. minced garlic
1 Tb. chopped cilantro or parsley
1 tsp. elote (corn silks)
1 scant tsp. salt
2 cups water or broth

Mole Soup

The blending of vegetables and chiles in a rich broth with shreds of meat creates a mole-like dish which is easy to make.

Simmer neck bones with bay leaf and a few peppercorns in 1½ quarts water for 2 hours or until the meat falls off the bone. Strain the broth and save. Bone the meat and keep for the soup.

Toast, strip and soak the chiles in 1 cup broth. Toast the tomatillos. Puree the oregano leaves, onion, garlic, cumin, tomatillos, and chile mixture in a blender. Slice the corn from the ear. Peel and cut the chayote into slender wedges. Peel the potatoes and cut into cubes. Snap the beans into 2-inch segments.

Bring the reserved broth to a boil. Add the chayote and the potatoes. Cook for 10 minutes. Add the corn and the snap beans and cook for another 5 minutes. Add the chile mixture and the meat. Simmer for another 10 minutes. Season with salt. Serve with lime wedges, cilantro sprigs and corn tortillas.

Makes 4 servings.

2 pounds pork or beef neck bones
1 bay leaf
Peppercorns
2 dried ancho chiles
2 dried pasilla chiles
Quajillos or negro chile (optional)
4 tomatillos
1 sprig oregano
½ medium onion, peeled and chopped
3 cloves garlic, chopped
½ tsp. cumin seed, ground
1 ear of corn
1 chayote (see COOK'S NOTE on page 80)
2 small fresh potatoes
2 cups snap beans
Salt

Mole Sauce

*S*erve with grilled fowl or cooked vegetables. It is especially good with grilled or roasted eggplant.

1 dried mulato chile
1 dried ancho chile
2 cups chicken or turkey
  broth
8 almonds
2 cloves garlic
⅓ onion, chopped
3 Tb. vegetable oil
3 large tomatillos
1 red bell pepper,
  chopped
1½ Tb. unsalted peanut
  butter
1 corn tortilla,
  shredded
½ to 1 tsp. salt

Toast chiles, then soak in 1 cup broth for 10 minutes. Cook almonds, garlic and onion in oil for about 3 minutes. Toast tomatillos until seared. Puree chiles and tomatillos in a blender. Add to the blender the almonds, garlic and onion. Add the bell pepper, peanut butter, shredded corn tortilla and salt to the other ingredients. Blend all together. Mixture should be very smooth. Return to skillet and simmer over low heat for 5 minutes.

Makes 2 cups.

COOK'S NOTE:

Chayote, also called christophine or brionne in French-speaking areas, is a very bland, squash-like fruit. The skin is inedible and must be removed. It can be purchased at specialty produce markets and in French or Hispanic markets.

Whole Squab in Winter Nut Sauce

*T*his is our version of a traditional pipian. It is wonderfully rich and satisfying and is an occasion in itself. If squab is unavailable, try halved Cornish game hens.

With poultry scissors or a very sharp knife slit the squabs, but do not halve them. If using Cornish hens, halve them. Mash and finely chop 1 clove garlic; finely chop 1 slice onion. In a large frying pan, cook chopped garlic and onion in oil and butter or lard until translucent, then add the squab. Cook, turning frequently, until just golden.

Grind the almonds in a blender or food processor, add the pimientos, clove, cumin and 2 to 4 tablespoons broth, just enough to create a paste. Add the tomatoes, the chiles, another clove of garlic, 2 onion slices, and the lettuce leaves. Then add the cilantro, the thyme leaves and the squash seeds. Blend. Add 4 cups of broth and the golden squab to the mixture. Cook, uncovered, over low heat for 30 to 45 minutes. Add salt to taste. Serve with a salad of Belgian endive and bitter greens, thick slices of homemade bread, slabs of butter and a Nouveau Beaujolais.

Makes 6 to 8 servings.

6 to 8 squab or 3 to 4 Cornish game hens
2 cloves garlic
3 slices onion
1 Tb. vegetable oil
1 Tb. unsalted butter or pure lard
2 Tb. blanched almonds
4 large pimientos, seeded, cored and deveined
1/4 tsp. ground clove
1/2 tsp. ground cumin
4 cups chicken broth
3 tomatoes, seeded and cut into wedges
4 serrano chiles, seeded, deveined and cut into cross-sectional rounds
6 leaves romaine lettuce
4 sprigs cilantro
2 sprigs thyme
1 cup pumpkin seeds or 1/4 cup peanuts
Salt

Guacamole

One of the most common moles is guacamole, of which there are many variations. Our favorite follows, but remember that other ingredients such as parsley, scallions, tomatillos, other chiles or lemon juice may be substituted for the similar ingredients in this recipe.

1 serrano chile
2 cloves garlic
1 Tb. finely chopped onion
1 tomato, finely chopped but not skinned
2 avocados, soft but unblemished
2 tsp. chopped cilantro leaves
Juice of small lime
Salt
Tortilla chips

Peel, devein and seed serrano. Mash garlic and serrano in mortar and pestle. Add the onion. Add the tomato and mash slightly. Scoop out the avocado pulp. Mash with a slotted spoon or fork. Add the garlic, chile, tomato and onion mixture. Add the chopped cilantro, lime juice and salt to taste. Serve with tortilla chips.

Makes 1 to 1½ cups.

Chiles in New Frontiers

Chiles are commonly thought of as indigenous to Mexican, Southeast Asian and regional Chinese cooking; as ingredients in Indian curries; as anathema to French and northern European cuisine; and only incidental to the cuisines of southern Europe and the Mediterranean, with the exception of North Africa. In this chapter we explore and provide some guidelines for taking chiles into unfamiliar culinary territories and incorporating them into some favorite dishes that normally do not use chiles.

Chile Heat

Chiles can add a fiery heat or a subtle piquancy to all sorts of dishes. Not all chiles are equally hot, and the characteristic hotness of the various kinds can be controlled, much the way the strength of garlic can be regulated by preparation and the timing of its addition to the cooking process.

Quantity. More chiles result in a more fiery dish.

Timing. As discussed in the Cooking with Fresh Chiles chapter, using a whole chile for a short period of time will provide an underlying flavor without making the dish too hot. Using a small amount of chile, seeded and deveined, will add another degree or two of hotness. Quick cooking, as in a stir-fry, will flavor and "heat" other ingredients. If desired, the chiles can be removed after cooking. Simmering chiles for a long period results in a product that is hot overall.

Size. Small pieces of cut-up chiles lend a uniform hotness to a dish. This is also true of chiles that are blended into sauces. Larger chunks of chiles remain as units and may be separated more easily from a dish than small pieces. When flavoring beans or soup, use two or three whole chiles, then retrieve them before serving.

Raw chiles are considered by most people to be hotter than cooked chiles. As discussed in the Cooking with Fresh Chiles chapter, salsas are frequently made with raw ingredients, then cooked. The same sauce may also be made, then not cooked at all, and the flavors as well as the hotness level will be subtly different. In Jalapeno Ice (page 100), roasted jalapenos are used, but you might try using raw ones instead for a different taste.

Vinegar and salt. Soaking fresh or dried chiles in a solution of 3 parts vinegar to 1 part salt for 1 hour will help to reduce hotness. Rinse thoroughly before using and dry. Then proceed with your recipe. Cream sauces are not a traditional part of Mexican or Southwestern cooking, but innovative chefs and cooks are using chiles to accent cream and wine sauces. These are lighter than the classic French sauces because they contain little or no butter and no flour. Try serving a jalapeno-accented cream sauce with scallops and squid over pasta. The chile is left in just long enough to infuse the sauce with its flavor and heat, but not long enough to dominate the sauce.

The cooling edge. To mitigate chile hotness use complementary ingredients as part of the dish, as condiments or in a sauce. Innovations with chiles require one to reflect upon the complementary ingredients that are used with chiles in their traditional cuisines. In Thai meals, sauces and entrees are served with cooling cucumbers and vinegars. In Mexico, limes, fresh fruits, cilantro and beer all attenuate chile hotness. Tortillas and cream absorb and enhance chile flavors while also acting as coolants. In India, fruit chutneys, limes, rice and breads serve the same role. In North Africa the volatile harissa served with couscous is balanced by the sweet, plumped raisins in the semolina.

Chile Pastries

Asian filled pastries truly lend themselves to cross-cultural concepts. The light pastries are made with wonton or pot-sticker skins which are easy to work with. Wonton skins and, often, pot-sticker skins can be bought ready-made at almost any market. The pastries can be steamed, boiled or deep-fried after being filled, and the method you choose can enhance your filling. For example, a very smooth filling might be complemented by a deep-fried skin; a crunchy, chunky filling by a smooth boiled or steamed skin. For serving, keep in mind too the concept of contrasts, the yin and yang of tastes. Pastries filled with chile-spiced ingredients are perfect to use with cool dipping sauces. Or do the reverse. Using a mild filling, provide a spicy dipping sauce. A good all-purpose dipping sauce, Asian in origin, uses cucumbers, white vinegar, Thai chiles, cilantro and a sprinkling of toasted, chopped peanuts. Just as versatile is a clear mint sauce made from white vinegar, mint leaves, jalapenos and sugar. Both sauces are light and good to serve with a deep-fried pastry as an hors d'oeuvre.

Sauces made with dried chiles tend to be rich and thick and are best used when the pastry is to be a substantial part of the meal or a full course. The combination is delicious, but filling. Also fresh salsas and deep-fried pastries make a good alternative to chips and salsas. The pastries can be prepared ahead, then deep-fried in shifts after the guests arrive.

Roast Pork Roll with Chile-Glazed Prunes

The flavorsome combination of roast pork and prune is amplified by the addition of negro chile powder and fresh herbs.

Spread boned roast open on a flat, clean surface. With a very sharp knife, slit through the thickness to within ¾ inch of the edge. Spread it open like a butterfly. Pat dry. Rub inside with 1 teaspoon salt, ¼ teaspoon pepper and ¼ teaspoon of negro chile powder.

To glaze the dried prunes, cook them for 3 minutes in ½ cup water. Reserve the liquid. There should be no more than ½ cup; if there is less, add a little water. Add the sugar, all but 1 tablespoon chile powder and the oregano to the prunes. Cook about 15 minutes, turning frequently. Be careful not to burn. Remove the prunes from pan when they are nicely glazed. Cool, cut each prune into 4 pieces and arrange them on the inside of the flattened pork roast, to within ½ inch of long ends.

Preheat the oven to 350° F.

Roll the roast carefully and tie with heavy kitchen string. Gently rub the outside of the rolled roast with salt, pepper and the remaining 1 tablespoon chile powder. Thin the remaining glaze from the prune pan with a little water and drizzle on the roast. Roast for 1½ to 2 hours or until done.

When the roast is done, let it stand for 10 minutes before slicing. Then using a very sharp knife, cut the roast into ½-inch-thick slices. Each slice will be a lovely pinwheel. Top each with crème fraîche and garnish with mint leaves.

Makes 6 to 8 servings.

5- to 6-pound pork loin or butt roast, boned
Salt and freshly ground black pepper
3 Tb. negro chile powder
12 dried prunes, pits removed
1 Tb. sugar
1 tsp. ground oregano
½ cup crème fraîche
Mint leaves, for garnish

Smothered Roast

A fond memory for many people is grandmother's smothered steak — a good round steak or chuck roast — covered with heaps of translucent onions which have been cooked in butter. This version uses mild green chiles and finely chopped onions.

5- to 6-pound chuck
   roast
6 Anaheim chiles,
   seeded and deveined
   (roasting is optional)
2 large onions, peeled
2 cloves garlic, peeled
1 Tb. freshly ground
   cumin
1 Tb. butter
½ cup chicken broth
Salt and pepper, to taste

Preheat oven to 325° F.

Dry roast and sear the meat in a heavy skillet over high heat. Turn. When brown on both sides, remove to ovenproof baking dish. Set aside.

Combine chiles, onion, garlic and cumin in a blender or food processor and chop. Melt butter in frying pan. Lightly sauté chile mixture in the butter until onions are translucent. Add chicken broth and salt and pepper, then pour mixture over roast and cook in preheated oven for 1½ to 2 hours.

This dish gets better and better with reheating, so you may want to prepare a day ahead.

Makes 6 servings.

Black Bean Wontons with Jalapeno Circles

This dish is easy to prepare and surprisingly light. The beans cook down and then are pureed. The slice of chile is raw and gives a bite to the finished product, but doesn't dominate by any means. A good choice for sauce is Fresh Summer Salsa (page 34) or Jalapeno Mint Syrup (see page 101).

Rinse beans and let soak overnight. To cook, drain soaking water and replace with 8 cups fresh cold water. Bring to a boil and add the garlic, bacon, salt and pepper. Cook 2 to 3 hours or until the beans can easily be mashed with the back of a spoon. Drain beans and adjust for salt. Puree beans in a blender or food processor. Put a spoonful in the center of each wonton wrapper and top with a jalapeno circle. To seal, fold into a triangle and dampen the edges with a little water. Press firmly. Set aside on a lightly floured surface.

Heat oil in a wok, deep fryer or a deep frying pan. The oil should be at least 1½ inches deep. The oil is ready when a piece of wonton wrapper dropped in bubbles, but doesn't crisp. Reduce heat slightly. Drop in the filled wontons, one at a time. Do not overcrowd; they should not touch. Cook 1 to 2 minutes, then turn. Cook until just browned. Remove to paper towels to drain. Serve warm with desired sauce.

Makes 24 wontons.

1 cup black beans
2 cloves garlic, peeled
4 pieces bacon, cut into 1-inch pieces
Salt and pepper
24 wonton wrappers
2 jalapeno chiles, seeded and sliced into thin circles
Peanut oil

Ancho-Walnut Cream Tea Sandwiches

The whole concept of afternoon tea is eminently pleasing, and we like the idea of serving unusual sandwiches such as this one.

1 ancho chile, toasted, deveined and seeded

½ cup mascarpone cheese

¼ cup finely chopped walnuts

Salt

8 slices high-quality white bread, crusts trimmed, or thin slices of pound cake

Watercress sprigs, for garnish

Soak the chile in 1 cup hot water for 10 minutes. Drain. Puree in the blender or food processor. Add cheese and blend. Add the chopped walnuts. Add salt to taste. Spread the mixture evenly on 4 slices of bread. Add tops and cut into triangles. Garnish with watercress sprigs.

Makes 16 tea sandwiches.

Chile Fleck Pasta

*T*ry *this pasta anytime you want to serve an elegant dish that is quick and easy to prepare. The flavor of the fresh herbs and the pleasant heat of the chiles create a full and satisfying taste.*

Bring a large pot of lightly salted water to a boil.

Meanwhile, chop half of the mushrooms. Leave the rest whole. Heat the butter and half the olive oil in a frying pan and add the shallots and the chopped mushrooms. Sauté until the mushrooms are slightly browned, but not juicy. Add the crushed chiles, 4½ teaspoons of the fresh herbs and the rest of the mushrooms. Cook for 2 to 3 minutes. Add the white wine. Increase heat and cook for 3 to 4 minutes more. Add the rest of the olive oil and the optional chicken. Keep warm over low heat.

Drop the fettuccine into boiling water and cook until just done, about 5 minutes. Drain and put pasta in a large bowl. Quickly toss with the grated cheese, then pour in the warm sauce and top with the remaining herbs, salt and freshly ground black pepper.

Makes 3 to 4 servings.

1 cup oyster mushrooms

2 Tb. butter

¼ to ½ cup olive oil

2 Tb. chopped shallots

6 to 8 arbol chiles, crushed and most of the seeds removed

2 Tb. chopped fresh marjoram, thyme or oregano

¼ cup white wine

1 cup cooked chicken or game hen, shredded (optional)

8 ounces fettuccine

¼ cup freshly grated Romano cheese

Salt and pepper

Rocket, Feta Cheese, Tomatillos and Avocados with Ancho Dressing

*W*hen *you prepare this simply composed salad, you can't help feeling that anything which looks so lovely must taste wonderful. The ancho dressing is a deep rich red, and the rocket leaves a strong, dark green. Both are highlighted by the feta cheese. The flavors combine as well as the colors, and the textures and the final result are a stunning introduction to any meal.*

16 medium or 32 small
   rocket leaves
6 romaine lettuce leaves
¼ pound feta cheese
4 tomatillos
2 avocados
2 Tb. sesame seeds
Ancho Dressing (recipe
   follows)
Juice of 1 lemon

Wash rocket and romaine. Arrange on individual plates. Slice feta into ¼-inch pieces. Cut tomatillos and avocados into thin slices. Divide into equal portions and arrange on the plates. Toast sesame seeds in a dry skillet over medium heat. Be careful not to burn. Drizzle the ancho dressing and the lemon juice over the salads, then top with a few sprinkles of sesame seeds.

   Makes 4 servings.

ANCHO DRESSING

Thin Ancho Salsa (page 53) with ¼ to ½ cup light vegetable oil such as corn or peanut until it is the consistency you wish.

   Makes 1½ cups.

Colorful Potato Salad

*R*ich ancho dressing combined with blue and yellow potatoes gives a wonderful appearance to a very tasty potato
salad.

Gently wash and dry potatoes. Do not remove skins. Boil or
steam potatoes until tender. Let cool. Remove skins if you
wish, and dice. Place in mixing bowl. Add onion. Cut half of
the pepper rounds into ¼-inch bits and add to the mixture.
Add celery, sage, oregano, mayonnaise and half of the Ancho
Dressing. Adjust seasonings, adding salt and pepper to taste.

Wash lettuce and pat leaves dry. Arrange 2 to 3 leaves
on individual plates. Place some potato salad on the lettuce.
Garnish the top of each salad with sliced pepper, an olive,
and a bit of cilantro. Drizzle with the remaining dressing and
add a dash of chile powder.

Makes 6 servings.

4 medium blue potatoes
   (see COOK'S NOTE)
6 yellow Finn potatoes
   (see COOK'S NOTE)
½ red onion, finely
   sliced
1 red bell pepper,
   seeded and cut into
   rounds
½ cup celery, cut into
   small cubes
1 Tb. fresh sage leaves,
   roughly chopped
½ tsp. fresh oregano
   leaves, roughly
   chopped
½ cup mayonnaise
¾ cup Ancho Dressing
   (see page 92)
Salt and pepper
1 head butter lettuce
6 green olives
2 Tb. chopped cilantro
   leaves
1 or more tsp. ancho
   chile powder

COOK'S NOTE:

Blue potatoes, also called purple potatoes, have a deep bluish
purple skin and a slightly bluish purple meat. There are
many different strains. In taste they are similar to a freshly
harvested baking potato.

Finn or Finnish potatoes have a yellow waxy flesh and
are quite sweet. They hold their shape well and are a good
salad potato. Look for both varieties in large supermarkets,
farmers' markets and specialty produce shops.

Cassoulet with Fresh Beans and Poblanos

Not a true cassoulet at all, this dish is nevertheless inspired by the traditional shelled bean dish of southeastern France.

1 large or 2 small ducks (preferably Moscovy with some fat)

2 cloves garlic, peeled

1 onion, peeled

¼ cup salt pork, diced and blanched, or lardons

4 large ripe tomatoes, skins removed and cut into quarters

3 sprigs fresh thyme

2 sprigs fresh winter savory

1 bay leaf

2 poblano chiles

4 cups fresh shelled beans (preferably cranberry type)

6 mild Italian sausages, cooked

Salt and pepper

GARNISH

6 basil leaves, chopped

2 whole cloves garlic

4 Tb. virgin olive oil

½ cup fresh bread crumbs

Cut duck into small pieces. Lightly sauté duck in large sauté pan or casserole. Add garlic, onion and salt pork or lardons. Cook for 5 minutes then add tomatoes and herbs.

Roast, peel, devein and seed chiles. Cut into strips ¼-inch wide. Reserve.

Cover and cook duck over low heat for 2½ to 4 hours until meat falls off the bone. This may be done on top of the stove or in the oven. Add beans and barely cover with water. Add sausages and cook, uncovered, for 20 minutes more or until beans are done. Add poblano chile strips and salt and pepper to taste.

To prepare garnish, combine basil and garlic in a mortar or food processor and crush or blend. Then add enough olive oil to make a paste. Spread bread crumbs over surface of cassoulet. Then sprinkle with garlic-basil mixture. Place under broiler just to brown bread crumbs.

Makes 12 servings.

Dandelion Greens with Roasted Poblano Strips

*T*he earthy taste of this dish—slightly bitter, slightly hot—is perfect served with a rich buttery background of polenta accompanied by your favorite spicy sausage. If available, chicory greens make an excellent substitute for the dandelions, and spinach will do if you can't find either.
This recipe lends itself to many adaptations—additional vegetables and meats are easily added for a hearty main dish, or use the mixture as a filling for lasagne, raviolis or burritos.

Carefully wash the greens but do not dry them. Without oil, cook the greens in a covered frying pan for 3 to 5 minutes or until just limp. Remove the lid, stir until the liquid has evaporated, then chop into 3-inch pieces. Set aside.

Roast, peel, seed and devein the chiles. Cut into strips ½-inch wide. Chop the tomatoes, the onion, and the garlic into small pieces and cook in the oil until soft. Increase heat and reduce liquid by a third, stirring constantly. Add salt and pepper to taste, then the chile slices and finally the greens.

Makes 6 servings.

1 pound dandelion
  greens
2 poblano chiles
2 very ripe tomatoes
1 onion, peeled
2 cloves garlic, peeled
1 Tb. light vegetable oil
Salt and pepper

Fiery Mussels

A *mix of Southeast Asia and southern France, this dish combines some of our favorite tastes and techniques, and is the perfect way to end a day of fishing and mussel gathering at the beach.*

2 to 3 pounds fresh
　mussels
6 or more arbol, pequin
　or tepin chiles
1 to 2 Tb. light oil (corn,
　safflower, or
　sunflower)
4 cloves garlic, grated
1 Tb. chopped onion
1 Tb. flour
1 cup chicken broth
½ cup white wine
¼ cup cilantro, chopped
Salt and pepper

Clean the mussels by washing them under cold running water and cutting away the beards with a pair of scissors. If they seem quite heavy with sand, leave them for 6 to 24 hours in a bucket of water, and they will disgorge the sand.

Remove the seeds and stems from the chiles and crush them into small pieces. Then, in a large heavy-bottomed pot, heat the oil and add the garlic and onion. Cook until the onion is transparent. Add the cleaned mussels, stirring all the while with a large wooden spoon. Sprinkle with the flour and the crushed chiles and continue to stir until the flour is no longer visible. Slowly add the chicken broth, stirring constantly. Finally add the white wine, the chopped cilantro, and salt and pepper to taste. Cover and cook about 10 to 15 minutes, until the mussels have steamed open and a nice sauce has formed. Serve with plenty of French bread or flour tortillas.

Makes 4 servings.

Chile and Sage Tossed Baby Potatoes

A favorite Italian way of cooking whole red potatoes is to rub them with olive oil, salt and pepper. Our combination adds chile and sage.

Preheat oven to 350° F.

Remove seeds from chiles and crush pods. Set aside.

Rub potatoes with oil, salt and sage leaves. Place potatoes and sage leaves in an ovenproof casserole dish. They should be closely packed. Dot with butter, add the cream and crushed chiles. Bake in preheated oven for 20 to 30 minutes, turning frequently. Add grated cheese, mixing it into the cream. Bake another 10 minutes, continuing to turn. Remove from oven, slice potatoes in half, turn gently in the sauce and serve topped with pepper.

Makes 4 servings.

4 small dried arbol or pequin chiles
16 baby potatoes
¼ cup olive oil
1 tsp. salt
12 or more fresh sage leaves
2 Tb. butter
½ cup heavy cream
½ cup grated Romano cheese
Freshly ground black pepper

Blue Cornbread

The colors of this cornbread are enticing and the bread delicious. It is not sweet and it enhances other natural foods such as beans and wild greens.

1½ cups finely ground blue cornmeal (see COOK'S NOTE)

1 tsp. baking powder

½ tsp. salt

4 fresh Anaheim chiles, roasted, peeled, seeded and chopped

2 egg whites

1 egg yolk

1 cup crema mexicana

1 cup grated sharp yellow cheddar cheese

¼ cup cooking oil

Preheat oven to 350° F. Blend the dry ingredients. Place in mixing bowl. Add the chiles, egg whites and yolk, sour cream, grated cheese and oil. Place in a greased 8" square baking pan, and bake 25 to 30 minutes.

Makes 6 servings.

COOK'S NOTE:

Blue cornmeal is made from blue tortilla corn. Until recently the cornmeal was available only in and around Santa Fe, New Mexico, where the blue corn was grown by local Indians and other farmers. Today, look for blue cornmeal and blue corn flour in the specialty sections of supermarkets and in specialty food and cookware shops.

Chile Figs and Hazelnut Torte

The underlying hint of something mysterious provided by the chile and the rich ground nuts amplifies the taste of the figs. Good served with a hard sauce or very thick whipped cream.

Wash the figs, then pour boiling water over them and let stand for ½ hour. Add the chile powder and brown sugar. Cook mixture in a small saucepan with ½ to ¾ cup water (depending on size of figs) for 20 minutes. Puree the fig mixture; add the juice of half a lemon and keep warm over low heat, stirring occasionally. If the mixture becomes too thick, add a tablespoon or two of hot water. It should spread easily.

Preheat oven to 350° F.

To make the crust, process the hazelnuts and the walnuts together until medium ground. Add egg yolk, melted butter, sugar and salt. Blend. Press mixture into the bottom of a 10-inch torte pan with a removable bottom. Spread the fig puree evenly over the top, and bake at 350° F for 20 minutes. Serve warm with hard sauce or whipped cream, garnished with sprigs of mint.

Makes 12 slices.

15 dried figs
1 cup boiling water
1½ Tb. chile powder such as Chimayo or Colorado
6 Tb. brown sugar
½ to ¾ cup water
Juice of half a lemon
1 cup ground hazelnuts
½ cup walnut halves
1 egg yolk
2 Tb. melted butter
2 Tb. sugar
½ tsp. salt
Hard sauce or whipped cream
Fresh mint, for garnish

Jalapeno Ice with French Melon and Mint Sauce

In this elegant dessert or first course, combining the hot chile with cool melons and mint is an excellent example of using ingredients which temper the fiery jalapeno chile while enhancing its flavor. If at all possible, use a yellow watermelon rather than a red one. The color of the ice will be a beautiful pale yellow-green. When served with the deep orange, highly perfumed French Charentais melon and a spoonful of dark green mint sauce, both the presentation and the taste are remarkable.

2 cups water
¾ to 1 cup sugar
1 to 1½ jalapeno chiles, roasted, peeled, seeded and deveined
2 cups watermelon meat, seeds removed
Juice of ½ lemon
2 egg whites
1 French Charentais melon

Combine water and sugar. Bring to a boil. Cool.

In blender or food processor, puree chiles. Add watermelon meat and lemon juice. Puree. Strain and add to sugar and water mixture. Put into 3 freezer trays or a stainless steel bowl. Freeze until almost solid. Remove from freezer, break into pieces and mix with blender, food processor or hand mixer. Do not "overdo." The mixture should remain "icy." Beat egg whites until stiff, then fold into ice mixture. Return to bowl or trays and freeze until solid, about 8 hours. Serve with sliced melon.

Makes 6 to 8 servings.

Mint Sauce

T*his recipe is from* The New American Vegetable Cookbook *(Aris Books, 1985). It is quickly prepared, refreshing, and recommended with the Jalapeno Ice. The sauce will not keep, so if you want to make it ahead, use Jalapeno Mint Syrup (recipe follows).*

Chop the mint sprigs. Puree all the ingredients in a blender. Serve at room temperature or chilled.
    Makes ½ cup.

1 cup mint sprigs (about 1 bunch or ½ pound)
2 Tb. water
2 Tb. sugar
2 Tb. rice wine vinegar or distilled vinegar
2 small fresh hot chiles such as jalapeno or serrano, seeded and minced

Jalapeno Mint Syrup

U*se for dipping filled dumplings or wontons as well as for desserts. This syrup can be stored for several days. You will find it surprisingly versatile.*

In a saucepan, combine vinegar and sugar. Bring to a boil over medium-high heat. Allow syrup to thicken, cooking 4 to 6 minutes. Reduce heat. Add 4 mint leaves and 2 of the cut-up jalapenos. Simmer for another 2 to 3 minutes, until flavor is as intense as you desire. Strain mixture. Pour syrup into serving bowl or pitcher, add last jalapeno slices, and garnish with remaining mint leaves.
    Makes 1 cup.

1 cup distilled white vinegar
1 cup granulated sugar
8 to 9 sprigs mint
3 jalapeno chiles, cut into cross-sectional slices

Jalapeno Cream Chocolates

Molded chocolate is easy to make when you have the correct utensils and ingredients. This recipe, although divided into three steps, is neither difficult nor particularly tedious. One needs only to candy the jalapenos, make a fondant and, finally, prepare the chocolate molds. The result is unique and strangely tempting, as both chiles and chocolate are addictive.

1 cup water

2 cups granulated sugar

6 jalapenos, seeded, deveined, and cut into slender strips

¼ cup unsalted butter

½ pound sifted confectioners' sugar

3 Tb. ground nuts, such as almonds or walnuts

3 Tb. heavy cream

1 tsp. tequila

½ pound semisweet melting chocolate such as Tobler, Lindt, or Ghirardelli

To candy the jalapenos, prepare a simple syrup by combining the water and granulated sugar in a saucepan. Add jalapeno strips. Bring to a rolling boil and cook until mixture thickens and reaches 221° F. Remove from heat. With a slotted spoon, remove the jalapenos and place on a plate. When cool, cut into very fine pieces. Set aside. Discard syrup or use for another purpose.

Make the fondant by beating the butter until soft. Add the confectioners' sugar, nuts, cream, and tequila and beat until very smooth. Add the jalapenos. Set aside.

To make the chocolates, melt the chocolate in a double boiler according to package directions. Have ready a chocolate mold. When the chocolate is ready to pour, fill the depression of each mold and let slightly set. Add a bit of the jalapeno fondant to the center of each mold. Pour more chocolate over the fondant and let entire piece harden at least 10 minutes. Turn the mold over and gently tap to release the chocolates.

Makes 8 large molded chocolates (2-inch diameter) or 12 smaller ones.

Jalapeno Tart with Oranges

*T*he colors alone in this delicious tart make it worth the effort. Again, the chile flavors combine wonderfully with the citrus and the pastry crust. Try serving this either as a dessert or as a first course.

Combine glaze ingredients. Bring to a boil and simmer until thickened, about 10 minutes. Remove from heat and set aside.

Preheat oven to 400° F.

To make the pastry, work the butter into the sugar and flour in a bowl with a pastry cutter, or in a food processor using the metal blade. Add the water until the pastry forms a ball easily. Roll the dough out on a floured cutting board or pastry cloth. Press into a two-piece tart pan or tartlet pans and bake until done, about 12 to 15 minutes.

To make the filling, coat inside of warm tart with glaze. Arrange the orange slices evenly on top of the glaze. Return to oven for 5 minutes. Remove the tart and drizzle with more glaze. Serve at room temperature.

Makes 6 servings as a dessert, 8 as a first course.

JALAPENO HONEY GLAZE
2 Tb. fresh jalapenos, roasted, skins and seeds removed, and minced
1 tsp. minced fresh ginger
3 Tb. water
½ tsp. grated orange zest
Pulp and juice of 2 oranges
1 Tb. honey

PASTRY
¾ cup unsalted butter
1 tsp. sugar mixed with 1 cup unbleached all-purpose flour
2 to 3 Tb. water
1½ to 2 pounds Valencia oranges, thinly sliced with rinds intact

Recipe Index

Index

Notes

Notes